A
STANLEY KUBRICK
PRODUCTION

A CLOCKWORK ORANGE

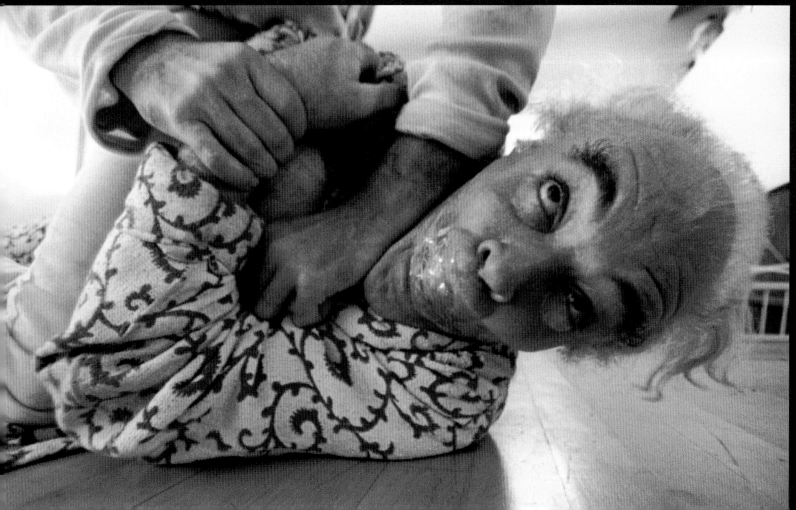

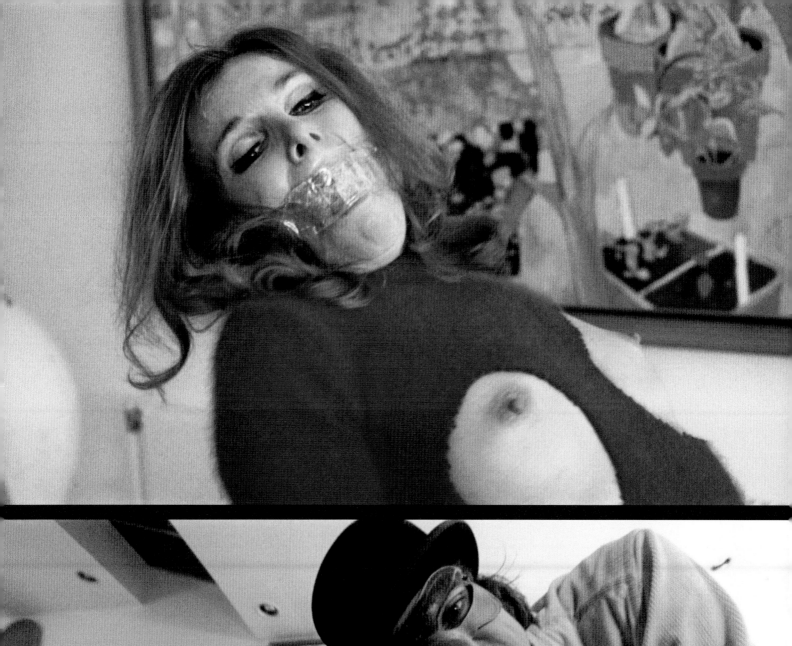

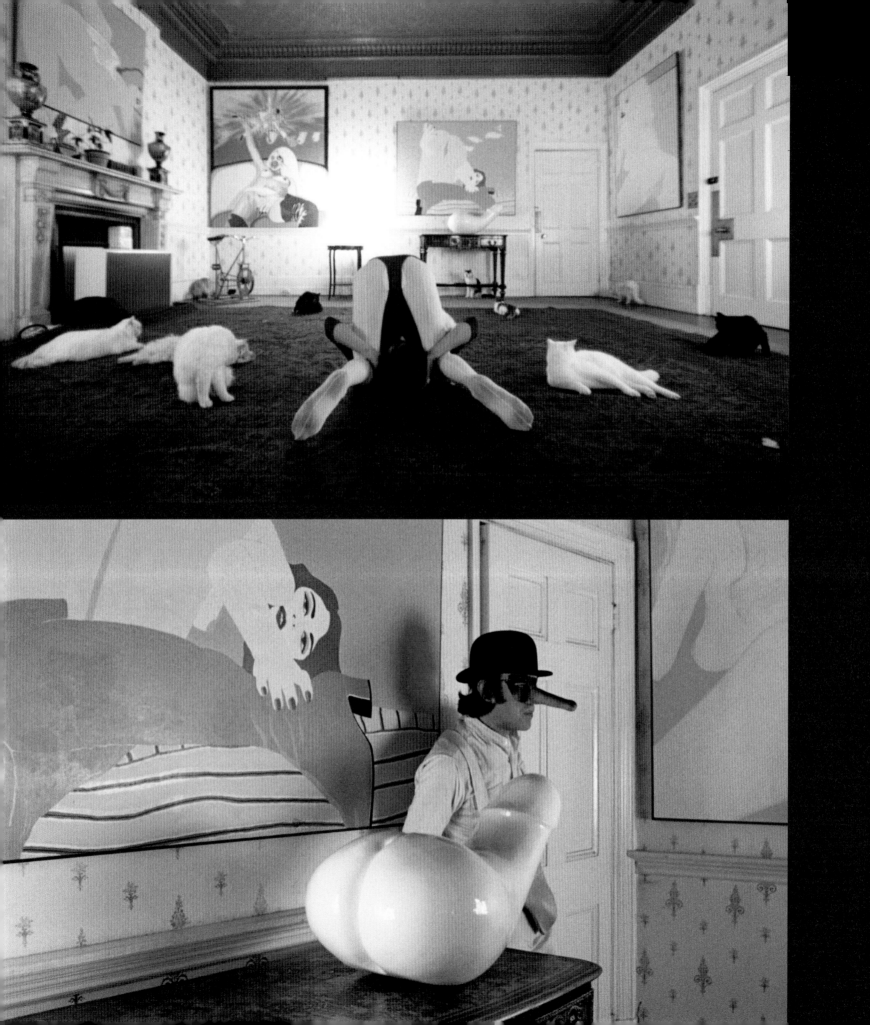

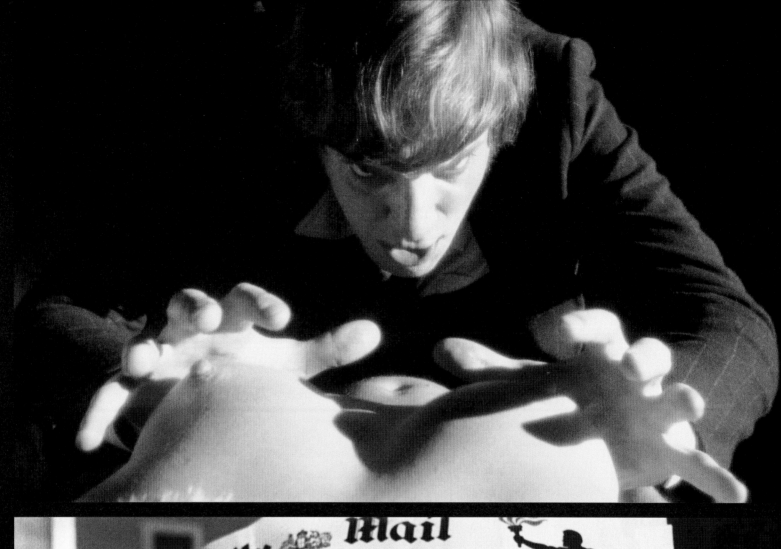

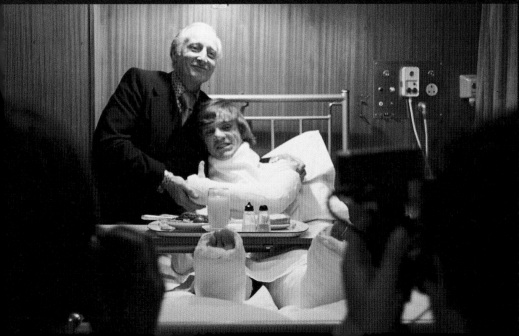
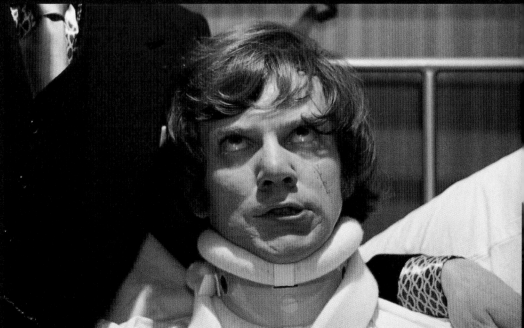

A CLOCKWORK ORANGE

1971 – Color – 137 minutes
Distributed by WARNER BROS.

CAST
ALEX Malcolm McDowell
MR. ALEXANDER Patrick Magee
DIM Warren Clarke
GEORGIE James Marcus
DELTOID Aubrey Morris
PRISON CHAPLAIN Godfrey Quigley
MINISTER OF THE INTERIOR Anthony Sharp
CHIEF GUARD Michael Bates
DAD Philip Stone
MUM Sheila Raynor
BILLYBOY Richard Connaught
MRS. ALEXANDER Adrienne Corri
DR. BRODSKY Carl Duering
PRISON GOVERNOR Michael Gover
CATLADY Miriam Karlin
TOM Steven Berkoff
TRAMP Paul Farrell
DR. BRANOM Madge Ryan
CONSPIRATOR John Savident
CONSPIRATOR Margaret Tyzack
PSYCHIATRIST Pauline Taylor
PETE Michael Tarn
LODGER Clive Francis
STAGE ACTOR John Clive

CREW
PRODUCED AND DIRECTED BY
Stanley Kubrick
SCREENPLAY Stanley Kubrick
BASED ON THE NOVEL BY Anthony Burgess
EXECUTIVE PRODUCERS
Max L. Raab and Si Litvinoff
ASSOCIATE PRODUCER Bernard Williams
ASSISTANT TO THE PRODUCER Jan Harlan
LIGHTING CAMERAMAN John Alcott
PRODUCTION DESIGNER John Barry
EDITOR Bill Butler
SOUND EDITOR Brian Blamey
ART DIRECTORS Russell Hagg, Peter Sheilds
COSTUME DESIGNER Milena Canonero
SPECIAL PAINTINGS AND SCULPTURE
Herman Makkink, Cornelius Makkink,
Liz Moore, Christiane Kubrick
CASTING Jimmy Liggat

ASSISTANT DIRECTORS
Derek Cracknell, Dusty Symonds
ASSISTANT EDITORS Gary Shepherd,
Peter Burgess, David Beesley
UNIT/PRODUCTION MANAGER Eddie Frewin
PRODUCTION ASSISTANT Margaret Adams
ADDITIONAL PHOTOGRAPHY Stanley Kubrick

Made at Pinewood Studios, London, England,
at EMI-MGM Studios, Borehamwood, Herts,
England, and on location in England by
Hawk Films Limited.

MUSIC
Electronic music composed and realized by
Walter Carlos
Ludwig Van Beethoven: Symphony No. 9 in
D Minor, Opus 125; Gioachino Rossini: *The
Thieving Magpie* and *William Tell* overtures;
Edward Elgar: *Pomp and Circumstance*
marches No. 1 and 4; Henry Purcell: *Music
for the Funeral of Queen Mary*
"Overture to the Sun" composed by
Terry Tucker
"I Want to Marry a Lighthouse Keeper"
composed and performed by Erika Eigen

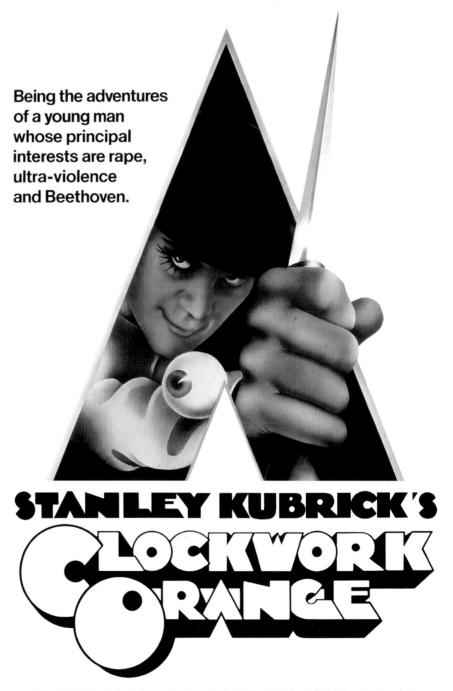

Being the adventures
of a young man
whose principal
interests are rape,
ultra-violence
and Beethoven.

STANLEY KUBRICK'S
CLOCKWORK ORANGE

A Stanley Kubrick Production "A CLOCKWORK ORANGE" Starring Malcolm McDowell • Patrick Magee • Adrienne Corri
and Miriam Karlin • Screenplay by Stanley Kubrick • Based on the novel by Anthony Burgess • Produced and
Directed by Stanley Kubrick • Executive Producers Max L. Raab and Si Litvinoff • WARNER BROS A WARNER COMMUNICATIONS COMPANY

A Clockwork Orange

by Michel Ciment

After finishing *2001: A Space Odyssey*, Stanley Kubrick turned to other projects, the first of which, "Napoleon," continued to obsess him for many years. To be produced —like *2001*—by MGM, it was abandoned because the major financial backing required for the production was not forthcoming; in addition, changes in MGM's management made the project even more problematic. Kubrick also gave some thought to a short novel by Arthur Schnitzler, *Rhapsody: A Dream Novel (Traumnovelle)*, whose potential had been spotted by his wife Christiane and which he brought to the screen some thirty years later as *Eyes Wide Shut*. But he was unable to develop a satisfactory screenplay for the Schnitzler and soon gave it up in favor of an Anthony Burgess novel recommended to him by his screenwriter for *Dr. Strangelove*, Terry Southern. This was *A Clockwork Orange*, on which Southern had taken out an option, adapting it for film with photographer Michael Cooper. Southern had then sold the rights to Si Litvinoff, his lawyer, and Litvinoff's partner, Max Raab. Kubrick signed a production deal with Warner Bros., with whom he was to work on all his remaining films, and bought the rights for $200,000 and a 50 percent share in all profits. "I was excited about everything about it," he said at the time, "the plot, the ideas, the characters and, of course, the language."

No great critical stir had greeted the publication of *A Clockwork Orange* in 1962. A difficult work for Burgess to write, it had a hideous autobiographical basis: his wife had been raped by U. S. deserters in London dur-

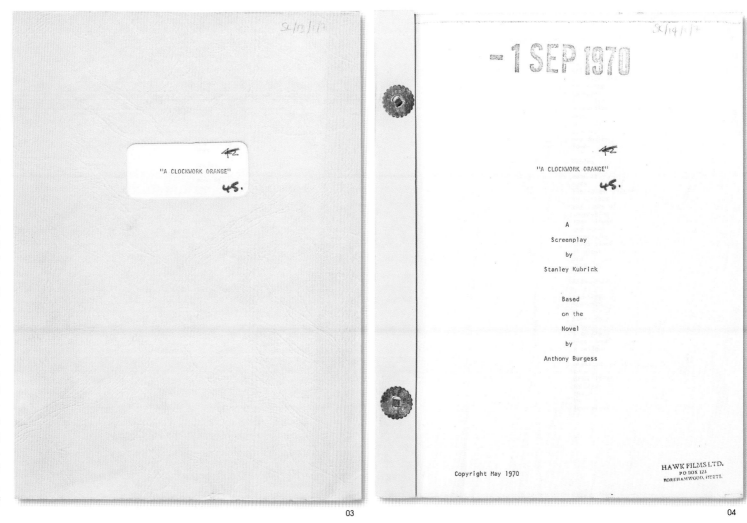

03

04

01 In this scene that was ultimately cut from the film, the droogs are shown stealing the car that they drive in the following scene.
02 The droogs speed through the night in a stolen "Durango 95." The car used was actually a 1970 Adams Probe 16, one of only three that were produced. The scene was shot with high-contrast footage projected in the background.
03-04 Working alone for the first time, Kubrick completed the script relatively quickly; the rights to Burgess's book were secured in early 1970, the first draft completed in May of that year, and shooting began in October.

ing World War II. The book formed part of a series of five novels written in quick succession by Burgess during a creative frenzy triggered by the discovery that he was suffering from a fatal brain tumor and had less than a year to live. In fact, he lived another twenty-five years.

This was the first film for which Kubrick wrote the screenplay single-handedly (*Barry Lyndon*, his next film, was the only other example of this). Of all the films that he made in Great Britain, these two are, paradoxically, the only ones whose cultural background is truly English. All the others, from *Lolita* to *Eyes Wide Shut*, are wholly American in both their settings and the nationality of most of their actors. The screenplays of both *A Clockwork Orange* and *Barry Lyndon* were, moreover, faithful adaptations of carefully structured narratives to which Kubrick made important but not radical changes. After working for four months—and using a computer for the first time, which enabled him to rearrange scenes digitally—he completed a first draft of the screenplay on May 15, 1970, using an unusual presentation: the action was described in the center of the page and the dialogue set out on either side. While shooting, from October 1970 to March 1971, Kubrick rewrote the dialogue extensively during long rehearsals with his actors and with Malcolm McDowell in particular.

* * *

A Clockwork Orange is set in England in the near future. The first scene takes place in the Korova Milkbar, where Alex (Malcolm McDowell) and his three droogs, Dim, Pete, and Georgie, imbibe hallucinatory drinks to stimulate their violent tendencies. They then attack a beggar and fight with their rivals, Billyboy and his gang. Finally they raid the isolated house of a writer and politician, Mr. Alexander (Patrick Magee), raping his wife. Alex then returns home to listen to his favorite music, Beethoven's Ninth Symphony.

The next morning, while his parents are at work, Alex is visited by Deltoid, a social worker,

Korova I   1

1   INT. KOROVA MILKBAR - NIGHT

                    Tables
                    chairs
                    made of
                    nude
                    fibreglass figures.

                    Hypnotic atmosphere.

                    Alex
                    Pete
                    Georgie
                    and
                    Dim
                    teenagers
                    stoned
                    on their
                    milk-plus
                    their
                    feet
                    resting
                    on
                    faces
                    crotches
                    lips
                    of the
                    sculptured
                    furniture.

         Alex: (Voice Over) There was me, that is
         Alex, and my three droogs, that is Pete,
         Georgie and Dim and we sat in the Korova
         milkbar trying to make up our rassoodocks
         what to do with the evening.

                                              9.7.70

05 *The stage directions for the opening shot mimic the long, slow retreat of the camera as it moves back from the closeup on Alex's face to reveal a wide shot of the four droogs.*
06 *The scenes in the Korova Milkbar were primarily lit by the bulbs in the pedestals of the milk dispensers, an economy that allowed Kubrick freedom to pan without having to worry about getting studio lamps in the shot.*

"The central idea of the film has to do with the question of free-will. Do we lose our humanity if we are deprived of the choice between good and evil?"

—SK/1972 (to Michel Ciment)

and later has sex with two young women he meets in a record shop. Alex and his gang, of which he is the leader, invade the house of the Catlady, who manages to alert the police before Alex kills her. He is arrested and sentenced to fourteen years in prison, but after two years he agrees to undergo the "Ludovico" treatment, a form of shock therapy administered by the government in an attempt to reduce criminality. The treatment consists of showing him violent images, such as Nazi war crimes, in an attempt to condition him to react with nausea to his own violent or sexual impulses. He also develops a revulsion to Beethoven, the music played as these images are shown to him. Incapable of violence after this brainwashing, he is released from prison.

He discovers that a tenant has taken his place in his parents' house, is attacked by beggars, and is beaten up by his former droogs (now policemen), but is unable to retaliate. By chance, he finds refuge with Mr. Alexander, who had read about him in the newspaper. To avenge himself and embarrass the government, he pushes Alex to attempt suicide by making him listen to Beethoven's Ninth. But Alex survives and, after hospital treatment, is declared "cured" of his brainwashing. The Minister of the Interior (Anthony Sharp) offers him a lucrative job, allowing him to give free rein to his recrudescent violence. The film's last image shows Alex fantasizing that he is making love to a naked woman in the snow before a group of spectators. He crows, "I was cured all right."

In the original English edition of the novel, the last chapter finds Alex fully reintegrated into society and living a peaceful family life. Kubrick, who became aware of the extra chapter in the English edition after working on the adaptation, nevertheless chose to use the American edition's ending, which better suited his deep pessimism and biting irony.

* * *

Considering the very slow, costly, and elaborate production of *2001: A Space Odyssey*,

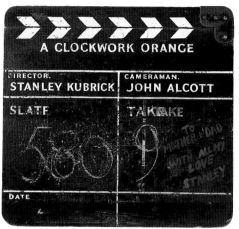

08

it is striking to note the small and extremely mobile crew used in *A Clockwork Orange* and the speed with which the film was made. For the first time since leaving the United States, Kubrick reverted to the methods of his earliest films, shooting for the most part in natural locations. Brunel University (later West London University) was the Ludovico medical center; the American drugstore on King's Road in Chelsea served as the location for the shopping center where Alex picks up the two young girls; the newly built Thamesmead area was used for the block of houses where Alex's parents live; South Norwood Library served as the auditorium where the press conference on Alex's treatment is held; the exterior of an Oxfordshire house was Mr. Alexander's home; and an old casino on Tagg's Island was the setting for the gang-battle. But Kubrick was never dogmatic, and constructed three sets in a disused factory in Borehamwood near the old MGM studios: the Korova Milkbar, the admissions room of the prison, and the entrance hall of the Alexanders' house. The Alexanders' bathroom was constructed under a tent in the yard of the Oxfordshire house.

07+09 Chairs and tables made of life-sized female effigies by the sculptor Allen Jones were the inspiration for the mannequin furniture and drink dispensers in the Korova Milkbar.
08 Kubrick gave the film's clapboard as a gift to his parents.

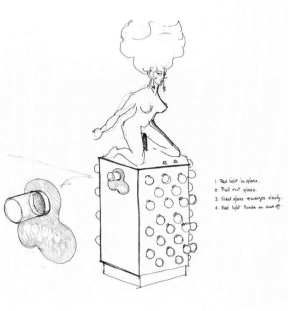

10

11

10 *Production designer John Barry's sketch for the milk-plus serving devices.*
11 *Liz Moore sculpts a mannequin for the Milkbar. Kubrick told Michel Ciment, "To get the poses right for the sculptress who modeled the figures, John [Barry] photographed a nude model in as many positions as he could imagine would make a table. There are fewer positions than you might think."*
12 *The Milkbar under construction.*
13 *The director demonstrates how to serve a glass of milk-plus.*
14 *Alex and droogs in the Korova Milkbar. Kubrick told* The Saturday Review, *"I had Malcolm McDowell in mind right from the third or fourth chapter of my first reading of the book. One doesn't find actors of his genius in all shapes, sizes, and ages."*

12

13

"I had seen an exhibition of sculpture which displayed female figures as furniture. From this came the idea for the fiberglass nude figures which were used as tables in the Milkbar."
—SK/1970 (to Michel Ciment)

15

16

17

18

A sense of urgency and dazzling flexibility inspired the filming. Having worked as assistant and additional photographer on *2001*, John Alcott was chosen as the cinematographer, though Kubrick as usual retained absolute control of the visuals. Giving up the 70 mm of *2001*, he adopted the 35 mm 1.66:1 format in an effort to avoid the "pan and scan" technique used for television broadcast. For the long zoom pull-backs of which he was so fond, he used an aperture of f 20.1. Conversely, the widest aperture setting of f 0.95 allowed him to work with natural light until very late in the day (unlike the f 2 he had previously used). He also set up a wheelchair for

the slightly elevated tight tracking shots in confined premises like the record shop visited by Alex and the prison visited by the Minister of the Interior. (This was one of his favorite stylistic techniques, much facilitated by the invention of Steadicam a few years later.) Often working with a hand-held camera—an Arriflex that cinematographer Haskell Wexler had tried out in his film *Medium Cool*—Kubrick could film within two meters of his actors and thus convey a striking impression of their physical proximity. (However, in *A Clockwork Orange* we also see Kubrick using experimental techniques rarely seen in his other films; for example, the orgy sequence was shot over twenty-eight

minutes at two exposures a second, lasting a bare forty seconds on the screen, while conversely, the battle between Alex and his droogs was filmed in slow-motion.)

The simple and straightforward techniques used for shooting were also applied to the soundtrack. Using miniature microphones worn by the actors, Kubrick recorded live sound and was a pioneer in using a new Dolby system in post-production to reduce or eliminate unwanted sounds.

* * *

A Clockwork Orange is, among Kubrick's films, the most directly linked to its period—to

its fashions, anxieties, and social and political concerns; its astounding mix of realism and stylization allowed it to reflect the spirit of the times without ever becoming bogged down in naturalism. Liz Jones, creator of the astral fetus in *2001*, collaborated with John Barry in the design of the Korova Milkbar, taking as inspiration the furniture-sculptures made by Allen Jones, featuring life-size effigies of fashion models, that Kubrick had seen in an exhibition. Two Dutch sculptors, Herman and Cornelius Makkink, created the four ceramic Christs (dancing as if in a musical comedy) that ornament Alex's room. The walls of the Alexanders' house and even those of the Catlady are decorated with contemporary

20

15 *Michael Tarn (Pete, left) and Warren Clarke (Dim, right) model various types of hats being considered for their characters' costumes.*
16–18+20 *These photos of Malcolm McDowell's costume fittings were taken at Kubrick's home in Abbot's Mead.*
19 *The droogs' rival gang, led by Billyboy (Richard Connaught, second from right).*

19

paintings—including many by Christiane Kubrick, whose large canvas *Seedboxes* is clearly visible.

Similar care was invested in the costumes, notably Alex's. Working with Kubrick for the first time, Milena Canonero had the stylistic sensibility the director was looking for. The bowler hat, false eyelashes on one eye, white jump suit resembling a cricketer's uniform, and the rubber codpiece make Alex into a dandy—a parody of the elegant and sporty Englishman. They also distinguish him from the character described by Burgess, who had a crew cut and wore black tights and hobnailed boots.

Kubrick successfully appropriates Burgess's narrative through his sheer visual inventiveness, which makes the film a unique and personal creation. From this point of view, the choice of Malcolm McDowell was essential since he worked very actively with Kubrick on both his "look" and dialogue improvisation on the set. Kubrick had spotted McDowell in Lindsay Anderson's *If* (1968), in which he played a rebellious teenager. The two men formed a close friendship despite

the fact that the filming proved very arduous for McDowell (his cornea was abraded in the scene in which a doctor administers eyedrops during the Ludovico treatment, his ribs were broken during the shooting of a public "re-education" lesson, and he was nearly drowned when his head was kept under water too long). Kubrick admired McDowell's vitality and humor, as well as the taste for extremity that he shared with Peter Sellers, Jack Nicholson, and Lee Ermey, setting him apart from another kind of actor favored by Kubrick: smooth and self-effacing types such as Keir Dullea, Ryan O'Neal, Matthew Modine, and Tom Cruise. Kubrick complemented McDowell with seasoned British stage and screen actors, a number of whom also went on to appear in *Barry Lyndon*: Patrick Magee, Philip Stone, Steven Berkoff, Godfrey Quigley, and Anthony Sharp. The

21+23 *Kubrick filmed but later cut a scene in which three colorful ladies in a café provide an alibi for the droogs when questioned by the police.*
22 *Costume test for Alex's droogs. Left to right: Georgie (James Marcus), Dim (Warren Clarke), and Pete (Michael Tarn).*

*"No one is corrupted watching
A Clockwork Orange any more than
they are by watching Richard III."*
—SK/1970 (to Michel Ciment)

23

"Writing a screenplay is a very different thing than writing a novel or an original story. A good story is a kind of a miracle, and I think that is the way I would describe Burgess's achievement with the novel.... A lot of fine novels have been ruined in the process [of adaptation]."

—SK/1970 (to Michel Ciment)

24 *A strong backlight was used for the scene in which the droogs attack a homeless man.*

**"To restrain man
is not to redeem him."**

—SK/1973 (to Gene D. Phillips)

scenes were created day-to-day as Kubrick improvised the action with his actors, taking as much time to rehearse as he deemed necessary.

He then spent six months editing, using two Steenbecks to select his shots as well as a Moviola. While making *2001*, Kubrick had discovered the possibilities afforded by existing music. Here he went further in this vein by asking the co-inventor of the Moog synthesizer, Walter Carlos (who subsequently underwent a sex-change to become Wendy Carlos), to compose electronic versions of Beethoven's Ninth, Rossini's *William Tell* Overture, and Purcell's *Music for the Funeral of Queen Mary*. As in *2001*, Kubrick makes use of contrasting music and images: the Ninth Symphony's exaltation of joy and solidarity is divested of any moral content by Alex, who hears it simply as an expression of vitality, and Rossini's *Thieving Magpie* accompanies scenes of ultra-violence between the rival gangs.

Kubrick gained control of the publicity for the United States launch of the film, after a standoff with Warner Bros. marketing management, thanks to the support of producer John Calley and the assent of Warner Bros. president Ted Ashley; Kubrick maintained this control for all his subsequent films. Since he was already guaranteed the final cut, he was now in a position to manage every stage of the making of his film—though still subject to the decisions of the censors. These were most severe in the United States, where no cuts were requested but the film was X-rated when it was released on December 20, 1971. Quality films were rarely rated "X" but in the months previous to Kubrick's release, John Schlesinger's *Midnight Cowboy*, Sam Peckinpah's *Straw Dogs,* and Ken Russell's *The Devils* had all suffered this fate.

The film's English première took place on January 13, 1972, after it had been passed by the secretary of the British Board of Film Censors, John Trevelyan. Kubrick himself withdrew the film in England in 1974 after he became aware of copycat crimes committed by droog look-alikes and received threatening letters. *A Clockwork Orange* was finally re-released on March 17, 2000, having not been seen in England for more than a quarter of a century.

The critics were, as usual, divided. *A Clockwork Orange* won the New York Film Critics award, but Pauline Kael in the *New Yorker* wrote, "How can people go on talking about the dazzling brilliance of movies and not notice that directors are sucking up to the thugs in the audience?" Andrew Sarris echoed this in *The Village Voice*: "See *A Clockwork Orange* for yourself and suffer the damnation of boredom." Vincent Canby in *The New York Times* took the opposite view: "Brilliant, a tour de force of extraordinary images, words, music and feeling. *A Clockwork Orange* is so beautiful to look at and hear that it dazzles the senses and the mind." Derek Malcolm in *The Guardian* shared his enthusiasm, describing the film as "A chilling and mesmeric adaptation of the Anthony Burgess novel which could well become one of the seminal movies of the 70s." Kubrick's peers immediately recognized his genius: Fellini, of course, who had always admired him, and Buñuel as well, who wrote, "*A Clockwork Orange* is my current favorite. I was very predisposed against the film. After seeing it I realized it is the only movie about what the modern world really means."

A Clockwork Orange received a number of Oscar nominations—including Best Director, Best Adapted Screenplay, and Best Film Editing—though it was *French Connection* that swept the awards. Despite a flurry of nominations, it was the same story with the Golden Globe and British Academy of Film and Television Arts (BAFTA) awards. However, it was hugely successful with the public. By 1979, it had already earned forty million dollars at the box-office—having been made for a mere two million dollars.

25–26 *This scene taken from Burgess's book, in which the droogs attack a professor, was cut from the film.*
27 *"I don't think I've ever had that much fun on a job.... The great thing that I think Stanley and I had in common ... was a wicked sense of humor." —Malcolm McDowell, 2001*
28–29 *Shooting the music bootick scenes.*

*"Although a certain amount of hypocrisy
exists about it, everyone is fascinated by violence.
After all, man is the most remorseless killer
who ever stalked the earth."*
—SK/1972 (to Paul D. Zimmermann)

SHOULD 'A CLOCKWORK ORANGE' BE BLAMED FOR VIOLENCE?

31

The film is the third part of a futurist trilogy and the *allegro vivace* third movement of a symphony after the *allegro* of *Dr. Strangelove* and the *andante* of *2001*. These films, through a combination of huge box-office success, philosophical debates, and controversies over the aesthetics, cemented Kubrick's reputation as one of the great directors of his time. His independence, the audacity of his projects, and his technical brilliance made him a major influence for the young American filmmakers of the early 70s—from Coppola and Scorsese to Malick and Spielberg, the pillars of the Hollywood renaissance.

Kubrick was unsatisfied with *Lolita,* and *A Clockwork Orange* represented his successful attempt to translate an author's verbal genius and wordplay (Burgess's invented language, *nadsat*) to the screen while presenting an accomplished example of a cinematic first-person narrative, something

Attack like 'Clockwork Orange' film

32

he had attempted previously in *Lolita* and later repeated only in *Full Metal Jacket.* The publicity slogan for the film, "Being the adventures of a young man whose principal interests are rape, ultra violence and Beethoven," is reminiscent of chapter epigraphs in 18th-century novels, and provides a clue to the orientation of the film: it is a philosophical tale *à la* Voltaire, a picaresque narrative in the manner of Fielding. In this respect it resembles Kubrick's next movie, *Barry Lyndon,* based on a novel by Thackeray, which was itself inspired by Enlightenment novels. The adventures of Barry Lyndon resemble Alex's in their division into two parts, the "conquests" of the first part being annulled by the failures in

30 *Kubrick with a 35mm Arriflex. He often did the camerawork himself, especially for handheld shots.*
31–33 *British newspaper headlines reporting on Clockwork copycat crimes.*
34 *The director lines up a shot from the Catlady's point of view as Alex prepares to strike her with a gigantic phallus.*

MURDER HUNT FOR 'CLOCKWORK' GANG

34

33

"I had Malcolm McDowell in mind right from the third or fourth chapter of my first reading of the book. One doesn't find actors of his genius in all shapes, sizes, and ages."
—SK/1971 (to Penelope Houston)

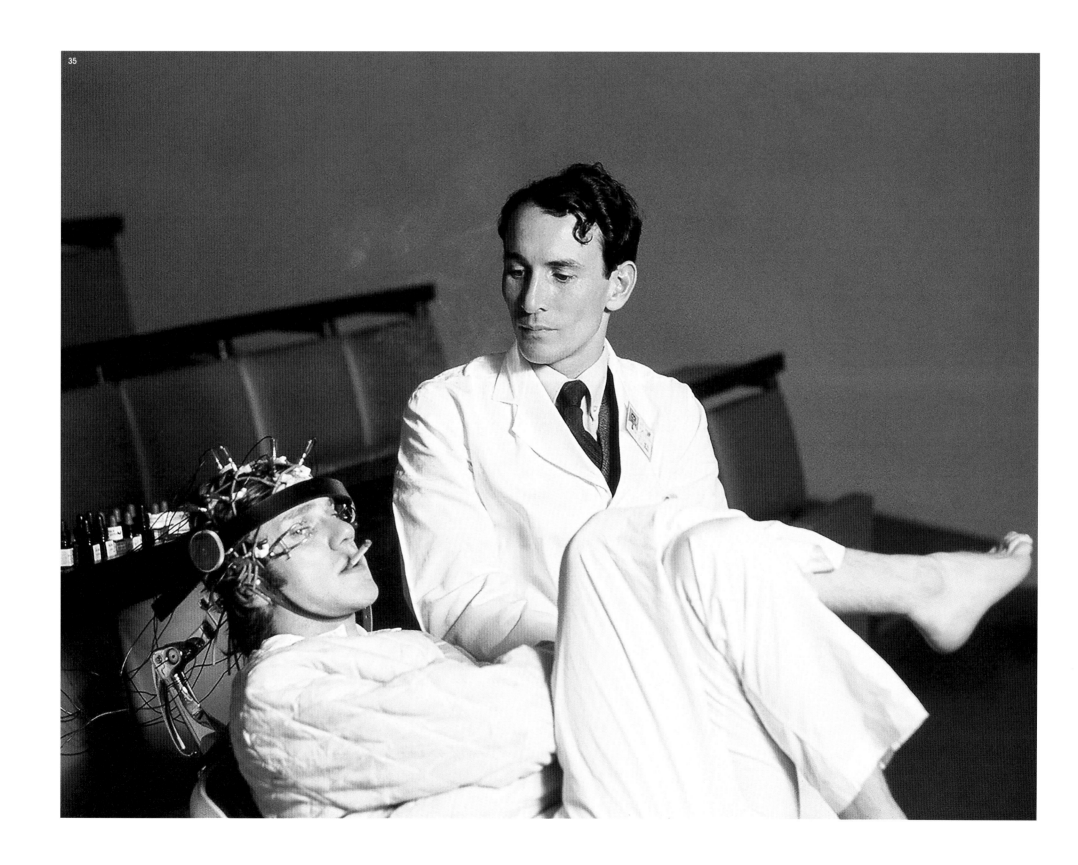

35

March 7, 1971

Narration

Then the film changed and I was heaving away but could not sick
viddying first a britva cut out an eye, then slice down the cheek,
then go rip, rip, rip, all over while red kroovy shot out onto the
camera lens. Then all the teeth were like wrenched out with a
pair of pliers and the creeching and blood were terrific. Then
I slooshied this very pleased voice of Dr. Brodsky going 'Excellent,
excellent, excellent'.

36

Now all the time I was watching this, I was beginning
to get very aware of a like not feeling all that well, and this I put
down to all the rich food and vitamins. But I tried to forget this, concentrating
on the next film which came on at once, my brothers, without any break
at all. This time the film like jumped right away on a young devotchka
who was being given the old in-out first by one malchick then another,
then another, she creeching away like very gromky and like
pathetic. This was real, very real, though if you thought about it properly
you couldn't imagine lewdies actually agreeing to having having all put
this done to them in a film, and if these films were made by the Good
or the Bad State you couldn't imagine them being allowed to take these
films without like interfering with what was going on. So it must have
been very clever what they call cutting or some such veshch. For it
was very real. And when it came to the sixth or seventh malchick leering
and smecking and then going into it, and the devotchka creeching on the
sound-track like then I began to feel sick.

Away like very gromky and pathetic

Topp

*I had like pains all over, and I
felt I could sick up, and at the same
time not sick up, and I began to feel like
I was in distress, Oh my Brothers.*

37

38

**35+38 For the experimental Ludovico
treatment, Alex is restrained, drugged with
nausea-inducing medication, and forced to
watch violent films with his eyes held open.
To shoot these scenes, McDowell had to endure
similar conditions (minus the drugs).
36–37 Drafts for Alex's narration during the
Ludovico treatment. McDowell recalled that
after shooting completed, "I had to come [to
Stanley's house] to do the voiceover for the narration…. He had a Sennheiser microphone with
a pencil and a rubber band so that I'd be the
same distance from the mike…. He was doing
it himself—no technicians, just Stanley with a
Nagra."**

"A lot of the problems of the human condition derive from an awareness of our own mortality. This is the curse of intelligence and language. No other creature except man has to deal with it."

—SK/1972 (to Gene Siskel)

HAWK FILMS LIMITED

POST-PRODUCTION.

DAILY PROGRESS REPORT No. 113

WEDNESDAY

PRODUCTION "A CLOCKWORK ORANGE" DIRECTOR STANLEY KUBRICK DATE 24 FEBRUARY 1971

STARTED	FINISHING DATE	SCENE NUMBERS
ESTIMATED DAYS	LOCATION OF WORK/SET	COMPLETED pick up shot on 40
DAYS TO DATE	INT. AUDIO VIZ	Probe under Trailer
REMAINING DAYS	Loc: Brunel University Uxbridge	PART 7:7.1:7.2
DAYS OVER / UNDER	EXT. MENACING CAR (REDUCED Loc: Colney Heath UNIT)	

TIME		SCRIPT SCENES						
			SCRIPT		EXTRA		RETAKES	
			NUMBER	MINUTES	NUMBER	MINUTES	NUMBER	MINUTES
CALL	9.00	PREVIOUSLY TAKEN	50	144.26			6	–
1st SET UP COMPLETED	5.35	TAKEN TO-DAY	–	–			–	–
LUNCH FROM	12.30	TAKEN TO DATE	50	144.26			6	–
TO	1.30	TO BE TAKEN	13	–				
UNIT DISMISSED	5.45				DAILY AVERAGES, OVERALL:			
" " Reduced Unit	11.30	TOTAL SCRIPT SCENES	63	115.43	STUDIO:		LOCATION:	

ACTION PROPS AND EFFECTS	SLATE NUMBERS	STILLS		
			B & W	COLOUR
robe 16	568-569	PREVIOUSLY TAKEN		
ork Trailer		TAKEN TO-DAY		
		TAKEN TO DATE		
	SET UPS: 2			

CONTRACT ARTISTES

NAME	W	S/B	RE	CALL	ARR	D'SS'D
MALCOLM McDOWELL				9.00	9.00	5.45

CROWDS

	RATE
Stunts:	
J. Wadham	30 – 00
A. Stuart	25 – 00
M. Boyle	30 – 00
2 Cr. Mrsls @ 15 – 00	
Additional Crew:	
R. Taylor (Operator)	27 – 00
D. Browne (Operator)	30 – 00
J. Morgan (Focus)	12 – 50
Mrs Emery (EEG)	16 – 00
Nurse	to be invoiced

Malcolm McDowell Voice Recording

Monday 1 March to Friday 5 March. A call was made for Sunday 7 March but was cancelled at 8.00 am as Malcolm was not feeling well. The recordings continued on Monday 8 March to Wednesday 10 March inclusive and completed. Malcolm was also called for shooting as noted above - Wednesday 24 February.

PICTURE				FILM FOOTAGES			SOUND	
WASTE	EXPOSED	S/E	TOTAL		PRINT	MASTER ROLLS	¼" TAPE	
39300	375670	13120	450960	PREVIOUSLY USED	224280		287 rolls	
580	1420	–	2000	USED TO-DAY	1600		1 roll	
39880	377090	13120	452960	TOTALS TO DATE	225880		288 rolls	
						WASTE:		

PRINT:
Previous: 281965
Today: 1260

Total: 283225

REMARKS

over ...

39

STOCK:

	CAMERA RM.	USED
1,000' rolls	6	83
400' rolls	39	451
200' rolls	7	123

CATERING: Lewis & Clarke - 60

CAMERA:
1 x Arriflex & 120 Blimp
1 x Governed motor
1 x 100mm lens   – Ronford
1 x 75mm lens

1 x 120 Blimp
2 x Samcine moy heads
1 x Cine 60 flatbase   – Samuelsons
1 x Elemack
Video camera, recorder & playback

PROJECTION: BP plate viewing at Pinewood Studios

TRANSPORT: Breakdown truck & mechanic (Ken Shepherd)

FACILITIES:
1 x Bessacar caravan
1 x Astral
1 x Catering Bus   – Andersons
1 x 3.5 A/C generator

ACCIDENT NOTE:
During shooting at Brunel University Malcolm McDowell had the lid clamps inserted into his eye sockets by our eye specialist Dr Gundry from Moorfields Hospital. During the take, which was covered by four cameras, the lid clamps slipped and Malcolm McDowell's left eye was scratched and the right eye suffered a slight abrasion. He was taken to Hillingdon Hospital by Dr Gundry for an examination and his eyes were treated with ointment and a pad was fitted on his left eye. We were advised that the damage was not serious and that Malcolm McDowell should go home and sleep ▆▆▆▆▆▆▆▆▆▆▆▆▆▆▆ and that he was going to have a fuller examination at 12.00 noon at Moorfields Hospital on Thursday 25 February. Malcolm McDowell went to Moorfields where he was examined and advised to rest and keep out of the lights as long as possible. This was in fact done and his eyes have now healed. I shall be obtaining a full report from Dr Gundry for the record.

CREW: (Brunel - B) All rates are ¼ of weekly salary.
     (Menacing Car - M)

TERRY CLEGG	– B/M	MAX HEUSSER	– B	EDDIE PRICE	– B/M
DUSTY SYMONDS	– B/M	DON BANKS	– B	SOUND BUS DRIVER	– B
VINCENT WINTER	– B/M	JOHN BARRY	– B	DR. GUNDRY	– B
JOHN HANSEN	– B	RON BECK	– B	CATERERS	– B/M
JUNE RANDALL	– B	GEORGE PARTLETON	– B	BILL WELCH	– M
JOHN ALCOTT	– B/M	OLGA ANGELINETTA	– B/M	PROBE MECHANIC	– M
JIMMY BAWDEN	– M	FRANK WARDALE	– B/M	RECOVERY LANDROVER	– M
RON RINKWATER	– B/M	LOUIS BOGUE	– B	TRAILER DRIVER	– M
LAURIE FROST	– B/M	DEREK GATTRELL	– B/M	JOE WADHAM	– M
DAVID LENHAM	– B/M	REG CARTER	– B/M	ALAN STUART	– M
DEREK BROWNE	– B	BOB LAPPER	– B/M	MARCUS BOYLE	– M
RON TAYLOR	– B	BOB HEDGES	– B	NURSE	– B/M
JOHN MORGAN	– B	JOHN PAYNE	– B/M	ARTHUR MORGAN	– M
TONY CRIDLIN	– B/M	RON COLDHAM	– B	2 ROAD CONTROLLERS	– M
JOHN JORDAN	– B/M	RON WARR	– B/M	BILL BEECHAM	– M
ROWLAND FOWLES	– B	BILL MONGER	– B/M		

BERNARD WILLIAMS
Production Manager

40

39–40 *Malcolm McDowell sustained injuries to his eyes during the filming of the Ludovico treatment scene, as documented in a subsequent daily progress report.*
41 *Despite suffering to get the treatment scenes in the can, McDowell was a good sport about it. Decades later, he told an interviewer, "Hey, listen, anything for art. Look what he did to my eyes."*

"I don't think that man is what he is because of an imperfectly structured society, but rather that society is imperfectly structured because of the nature of man. No philosophy based on an incorrect view of the nature of man is likely to produce social good."

—SK/1970 (to Michel Ciment)

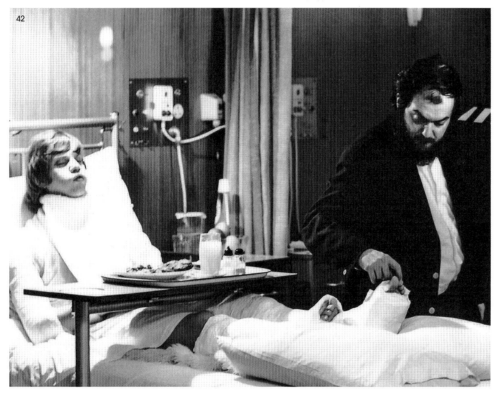

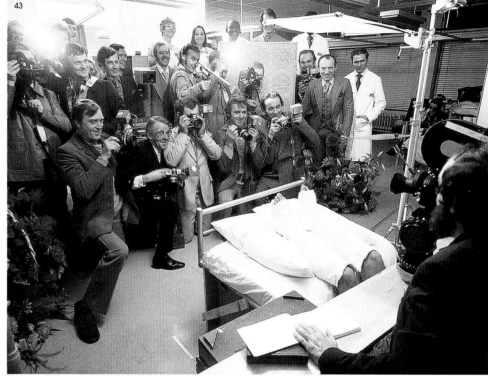

the second. The symmetry of construction in *A Clockwork Orange* is very striking, with a number of sequences from the first part mirrored in the second: the drunken Irishman attacked by Alex later gets revenge, as does Mr. Alexander for the destroying of his home and the murder of his wife; Alex dominates his droogs in the first part and is beaten up by them in the second, when they have become policemen; Alex lives at his parents' house in the first part and finds his room is occupied by a stranger in the second, after his release from prison. This circularity is underlined by a number of visual motifs: bowler hat, billiard balls, eye lined by false eyelashes, the prisoners circling around the exercise yard, and women's breasts. The accompanying symmetry is present in the opening sequence in the bar, in the mirror-filled bathroom of the Alexanders' home, and in the checkered floor-tiles. The very title of the work, inspired by the Cockney expression "queer as a clockwork orange,"

conveys the duality between the mechanical (clockwork) and organic (orange).

Kubrick's position is far from Burgess's Christian vision. In Kubrick's dialectical perspective, the State cynically salvages Alex for its own purposes and employs society's worst members to reinforce its control. In this respect, the film is faithful to the libertarian character of its inspiration, echoing the aphorism "no gods, no masters." From *Paths of Glory* to *Full Metal Jacket* and from *Dr. Strangelove* to *A Clockwork Orange*—not to mention *Spartacus*, which was not even a Kubrick project—he always denounced the coercive power of politicians and the military and even of scientists, all of whom he perceived as forcing the individual to conform. Alex embodies our spontaneous resistance to those who attempt to make use of us. His behavior fills us with horror and his ethics are contemptible, but he is human nonetheless. Alex exercises his free will to do evil against a society that also does evil—in the name

of morality. Kubrick implicates psychological conditioning as theorized by B. F. Skinner and reflects on the relationship between images and seeing.

The eye of Alex, actor and spectator of human decadence, as well as that of Mr. Alexander when he is forced to look on as his wife is raped, are the film's most striking manifestations of the power of sight. Moreover, Alex's own mental flashes are themselves steeped in Hollywood imagery: Alex as Roman centurion taking part in the flagellation of Christ, Alex as Dracula with dripping fangs, Alex as a biblical character surrounded by naked women and devouring grapes, and Alex violently beaten up as if in a Peckinpah movie. These film images are double-edged: they feed Alex's sadistic erotic fantasies, while for the State they serve as an instrument of surveillance and propaganda. Kubrick, criticizing the medium in which he works, has always favored distance over the character-identification

basis of the Hollywood approach. But he knows the perverse power of cinema: the wide angle reverse traveling shots that he so favors are a manifestation of repulsion and also a sign of fascination. Kubrick also filled *A Clockwork Orange* with references to his own films: the close-up of Alex's eye that opens the film echoes the eye of the astral fetus in the last shot of *2001*; the two *devotchkas* in the drugstore (which is selling a record of the *2001* soundtrack) are Lolitas with their phallic lollipops. The two stereophonic speakers in the hospital room evoke the black monolith of *2001* as a prelude to Alex's regeneration, while the final vision of elegantly dressed aristocrats anticipates *Barry Lyndon*.

In *A Clockwork Orange,* Kubrick, ever the orthodox Freudian, reaffirms the existence of the id and the dangers it represents, and is skeptical about the possibility of human progress. Alex, rising with his cane to bring his droogs into line, is filmed in slow-motion, from a low angle, like the ape of *2001* with his murderous bone-weapon. Violence is thus omnipresent, as is sexuality, which here is no longer subversive, as it was at the time of the surrealists, but is part of a fastidious and blasé celebration. Proof of this is found in the decoration of the Korova Milkbar with its statues offering the milk of artificial paradise, the phallic snake in Alex's room, the paintings and sculptures in the Catlady's home, and the obsession with breasts throughout the film. Homoeroticism also features in the sexual advances made by Deltoid to Alex, the latter's rectal examination by the chief warder, the emphasis on blows to Alex's testicles and penis (emphasized by his garments), and the rocking penis in the Catlady's house, whose décor is full of lesbian imagery.

Far from being a counterpoison to the excesses of nature, culture is impotent to constrain evil and even participates in it; Beethoven's music triggers Alex's destructive energies and is used in the very disturbing "curative" therapy he receives. Kubrick's outlook has never been as somber as it is in this film: hoodlums and police officers are interchangeable and the chief representative of the liberal opposition, who lives in luxury and despises the masses, is no better than the Minister of the Interior and his smooth-talking insincerity. Moreover, Mr. Alexander is in a sense Alex's double, sharing his name and his love of Beethoven (his doorbell sounds the opening theme of the Fifth Symphony) while resembling "Ludwig van" in his facial features and abundant mane of hair.

The negative dialectic of Kubrick's two most overtly comical films—the black farce of *Dr. Strangelove* and the biting satire of *A Clockwork Orange*—makes them the most powerful expression of a central theme in his work: the discontents of civilization.

42–44 *Filming the scenes of Alex recuperating in the hospital and enjoying the attention of the press, eager to cast him as poster boy for the government's inhumane treatment methods.*

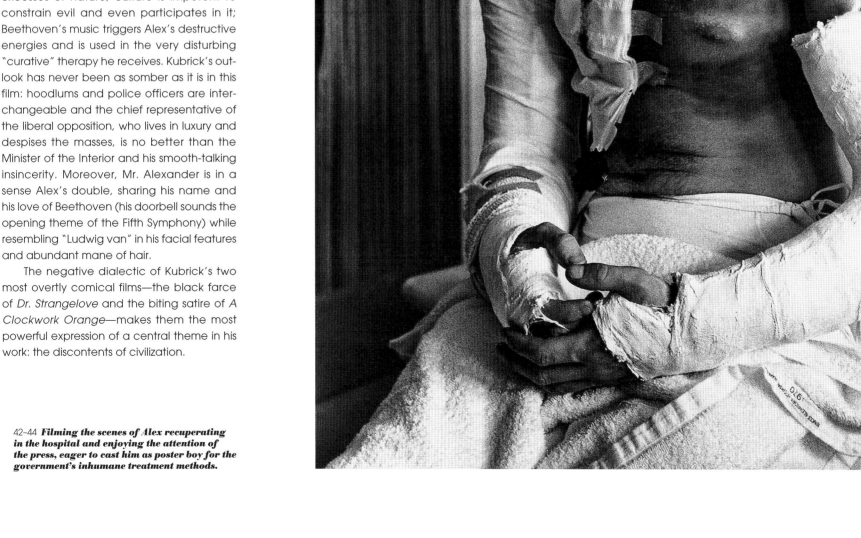

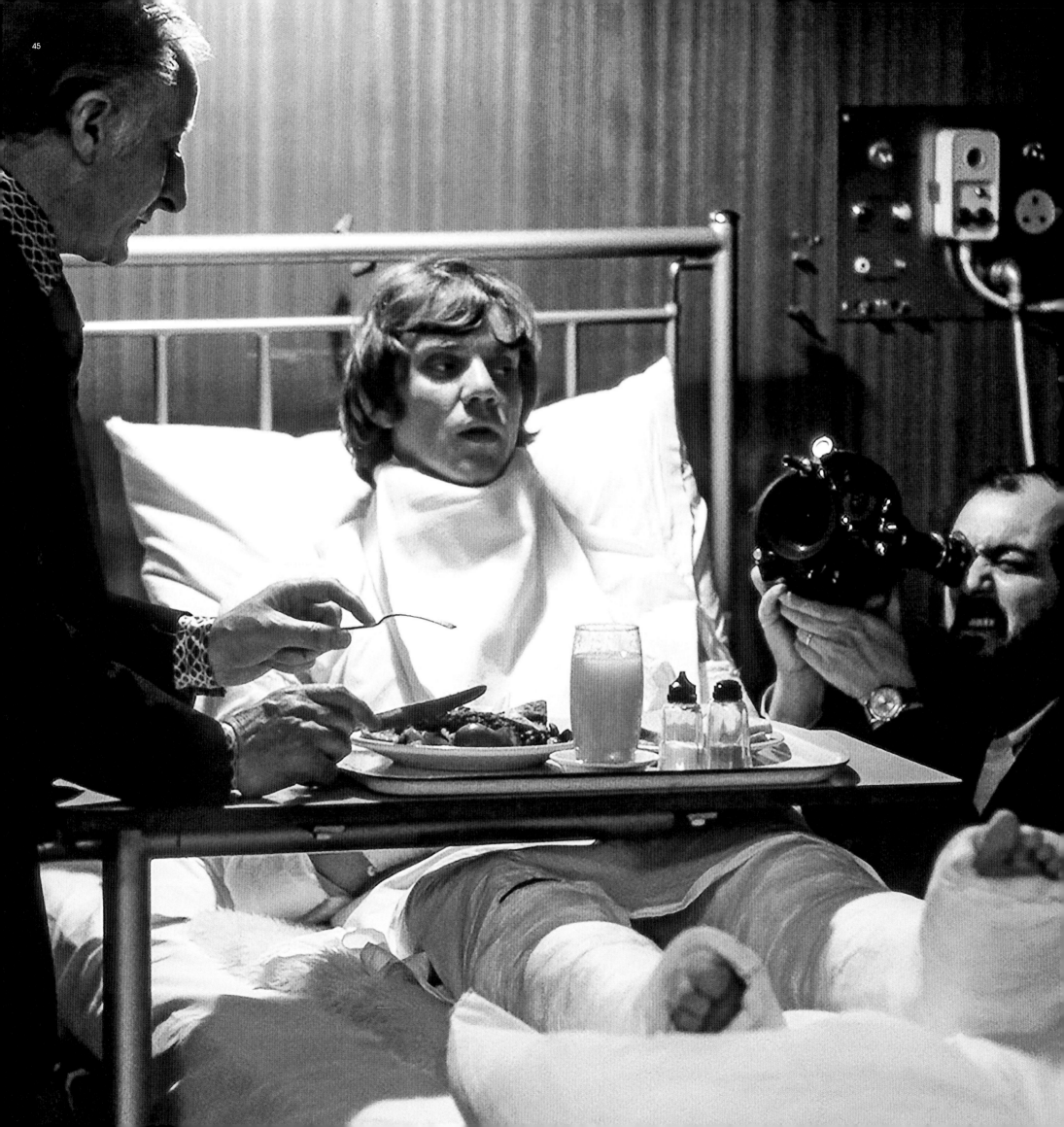

47

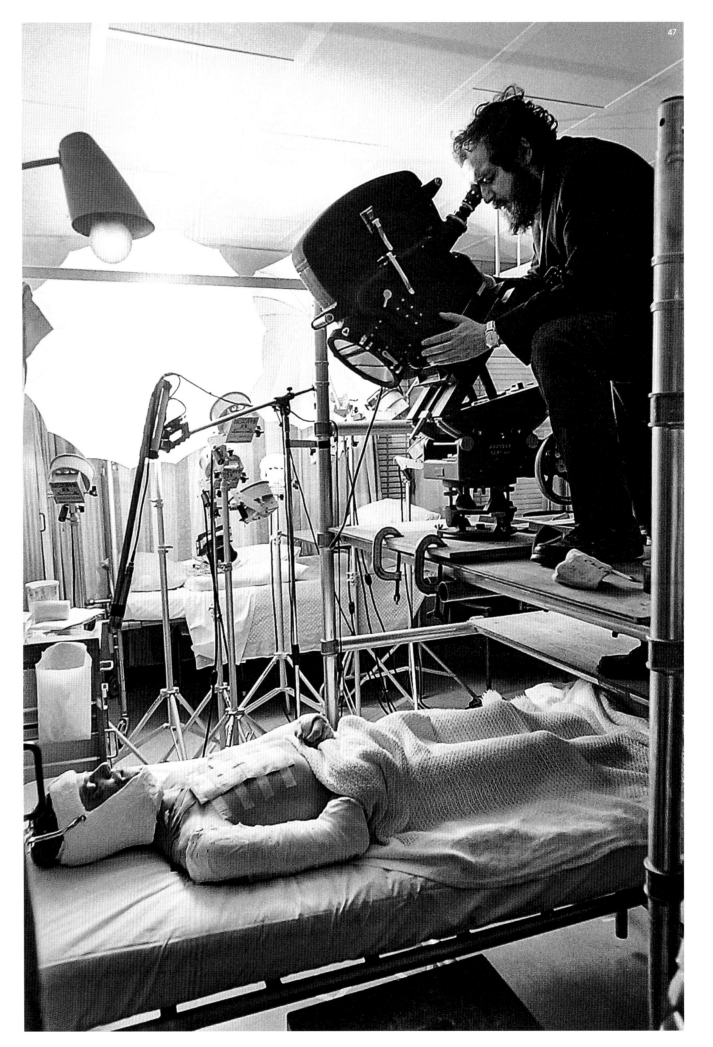

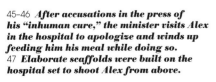

46

45–46 *After accusations in the press of his "inhuman cure," the minister visits Alex in the hospital to apologize and winds up feeding him his meal while doing so.*
47 *Elaborate scaffolds were built on the hospital set to shoot Alex from above.*

Letter to the Editor of *The New York Times*

by Stanley Kubrick

Published in The New York Times,
February 27, 1972

"An alert liberal," says Fred M. Hechinger, writing about my film *A Clockwork Orange*, "should recognize the voice of fascism." They don't come any more alert than Fred M. Hechinger. A movie critic, whose job is to analyze the actual content of a film, rather than second-hand interviews, might have fallen down badly on sounding the "Liberal Alert" which an educationist like Mr. Hechinger confidently set jangling in so many resonant lines of alarmed prose.

As I read them, the image that kept coming to mind was of Mr. Hechinger, cast as the embattled liberal, grim-visaged the way Gary Cooper used to be, doing the long walk down main street to face the high noon of American democracy, while out of the Last Chance saloon drifts the theme song, "See what the boys in the backlash will have and tell them I'm having the same," though sung in a voice less like Miss Dietrich's than Miss Kael's. Alert filmgoers will recognize that I am mixing my movies. But then alert educationists like Mr. Hechinger seemingly don't mind mixing their metaphors: "Occasionally, the diverting tinsel was laced with some 'Grapes of Wrath' realism," no less.

It is baffling that in the course of his lengthy piece encouraging American liberals to cherish their "right" to hate the ideology behind *A Clockwork Orange*, Mr. Hechinger quotes not one line, refers to not one scene, analyzes not one theme from the film—but simply lumps it indiscriminately in with a "trend" which he pretends to distinguish ("a deeply anti-liberal totalitarian nihilism") in several current films. Is this, I wonder, because he couldn't actually find any internal evidence to support his trend-spotting? If not, then it is extraordinary that so serious a charge should be made against it (and myself) inside so fuzzy and unfocussed a piece of alarmist journalism.

* * *

Hechinger is probably quite sincere in what he feels. But what the witness feels, as the judge said, is not evidence—the more so when the charge is one of purveying "the essence of fascism."

"Is this an uncharitable reading of the film's thesis?" Mr. Hechinger asks himself with unwonted, if momentary doubt. I would reply that it is an *irrelevant* reading of the thesis, in fact an insensitive and inverted reading of the thesis, which, so far from advocating that fascism be given a second chance, warns against the new psychedelic fascism—the eye-popping, multimedia, quadrasonic, drug-oriented conditioning of human beings by other beings—which many believe will usher in the forfeiture of human citizenship and the beginning of zombiedom.

* * *

It is quite true that my film's view of man is less flattering than the one Rousseau entertained in a similarly allegorical narrative—but, in order to avoid fascism, does one have to view man as a *noble* savage, rather than an ignoble one? Being a pessimist is not yet enough to qualify one to be regarded as a tyrant (I hope). At least the film critic of *The New York Times*, Vincent Canby, did not believe so. Though modestly disclaiming any theories of initial causes and long range effects of films—a professional humility that contrasts very markedly with Mr. Hechinger's lack of the same—Mr. Canby nevertheless classified *A Clockwork Orange* as "a superlative example" of the kind of movies that "seriously attempt to analyze the meaning of violence and the social climate that tolerates it." He certainly did not denounce me as a fascist, no more than any well-balanced commentator who read "A Modest Proposal" would have accused Dean Swift of being a cannibal.

Anthony Burgess is on record as seeing the film as "a Christian Sermon" and lest this

48 *On location for the prison scenes.*
49 *Prison chief guard Michael Bates with Kubrick and McDowell.*

50

be regarded as a piece of special pleading by the original begetter of *A Clockwork Orange*, I will quote the opinion of John E. Fitzgerald, the film critic of *The Catholic News*, who, far from believing the film to show man, in Mr. Hechinger's "uncharitable" reading, as "irretrievably bad and corrupt," went straight to the heart of the matter in a way that shames the fumbling innuendos of Mr. Hechinger.

"In one year," Mr. Fitzgerald wrote, "we have been given two contradictory messages in two mediums. In print, we've been told (in B. F. Skinner's *Beyond Freedom and Dignity*) that man is but a grab-bag of conditioned reflexes. On screen, with images rather than words, Stanley Kubrick shows that man is more than a mere product of heredity and-or environment. For as Alex's clergyman friend (a character who starts out as a fire-and-brimstone spouting balloon, but ends up as the spokesman for the film's thesis) says: 'When a man cannot choose, he ceases to be a man.'

"The film seems to say that to take away man's choice is not to redeem but merely to restrain him; otherwise we have a society of oranges, organic but operating like clockwork. Such brainwashing, organic and psychological, is a weapon that totalitarians in state, church or society might wish for as an easier good, even at the cost of individual rights and dignity. Redemption is a complicated thing and change must be motivated from within rather than imposed from without if moral values are to be upheld."

"It takes the likes of Hitler or Stalin, and the violence of inquisitions, pogroms and purges to manage a world of ignoble savages," declares Mr. Hechinger in a manner both savage and ignoble. Thus, without citing anything from the film itself, Mr. Hechinger seems to rest his entire case against me on a quote appearing in *The New York Times* of January

50 *Kubrick on location for the scenes in the Alexander home.*
51 *Kubrick on set with the droogs.*

30, in which I said: "Man isn't a noble savage, he's an ignoble savage. He is irrational, brutal, weak, silly, unable to be objective about anything where his own interests are involved … and any attempt to create social institutions based on a false view of the nature of man is probably doomed to failure." From this, apparently Mr. Hechinger concluded, "the thesis that man is irretrievably bad and corrupt is the essence of fascism," and summarily condemned the film.

Mr. Hechinger is entitled to hold an optimistic view of the nature of man, but this does not give him the right to make ugly assertions of fascism against those who do not share his opinion.

I wonder how he would reconcile his simplistic notions with the views of such an acknowledged anti-fascist as Arthur Koestler, who wrote in his book *The Ghost in the Machine*, "The Promethean myth has acquired an ugly twist: the giant reaching out to steal the lightning from the Gods is insane…. When you mention, however tentatively, the hypothesis that a paranoid streak is inherent in the human condition, you will promptly be accused of taking a one-sided, morbid view of history; of being hypnotized by its negative aspects; of picking out the black stones in the mosaic and neglecting the triumphant achievements of human progress…. To dwell on the glories of man and ignore the symptoms of his possible insanity is not a sign of optimism but of ostrichism. It could only be compared to the attitude of that jolly physician who, a short time before Van Gogh committed suicide, declared that he could not be insane because he painted such beautiful pictures." Does this, I wonder, place Mr. Koestler on Mr. Hechinger's newly started blacklist?

It is because of the hysterical denunciations of self-proclaimed "alert liberals" like Mr. Hechinger that the cause of liberalism is weakened, and it is for the same reason that so few liberal-minded politicians risk making realistic statements about contemporary social problems.

The age of the alibi, in which we find ourselves, began with the opening sentence of Rousseau's *Emile*: "Nature made me happy and good, and if I am otherwise, it is society's fault." It is based on two misconceptions: that man in his natural state was happy and good, and that primal man had no society.

Robert Ardrey has written in *The Social Contract*, "The organizing principle of Rousseau's life was his unshakable belief in the original goodness of man, including his own. That it led him into the most towering hypocrisies, as recorded in the *Confessions*, is of no shaking importance; such hypocrisies must follow from such an assumption. More significant are the disillusionments, the pessimism, and the paranoia that such a belief in human nature must induce."

* * *

Ardrey elaborates in *African Genesis*: "the idealistic American is an environmentalist who accepts the doctrine of man's innate nobility and looks chiefly to economic causes for the source of human woe. And so now, at the peak of the American triumph over that ancient enemy, want, he finds himself harassed by the racial conflict of increasing bitterness, harrowed by juvenile delinquency probing championship heights."

Rousseau's romantic fallacy that it is society which corrupts man, not man who corrupts society, places a flattering gauze between ourselves and reality. This view, to use Mr. Hechinger's frame of reference, is solid box office but, in the end, such a self-inflating illusion leads to despair.

The Enlightenment declared man's rational independence from the tyranny of the Supernatural. It opened up dizzying and frightening vistas of the intellectual and political future. But before this became too alarming, Rousseau replaced a religion of the Supernatural being with the religion of natural man. God might be dead. "Long live man."

"How else," writes Ardrey, "can one explain—except as a substitute for old reli-

gious cravings—the immoderate influence on the rational mind of the doctrine of innate goodness?"

Finally, the question must be considered whether Rousseau's view of man as fallen angel is not really the most pessimistic and hopeless of philosophies. It leaves man a monster who has gone steadily away from his original nobility. It is, I am convinced, more optimistic to accept Ardrey's view that "… we were born of risen apes, not fallen angels, and the apes were armed killers besides. And so what shall we wonder at? Our murders and massacres and missiles and our irreconcilable regiments? For our treaties, whatever they may be worth; our symphonies, however seldom they may be played; our peaceful acres, however frequently they may be converted into battlefields; our dreams, however rarely they may be accomplished. The miracle of man is not how far he has sunk but how magnificently he has risen. We are known among the stars by our poems, not our corpses."

Mr. Hechinger is no doubt a well-educated man but the tone of his piece strikes me as also that of a well-conditioned man who responds to what he expects to find, or has been told, or has read about, rather than to what he actually perceives *A Clockwork Orange* to be. Maybe he should deposit his grab-bag of conditioned reflexes outside and go in to see it again. This time, exercising a little choice.

52-54 *Script notes, dialogue, and set still from cut scenes of the droogs stealing a car, vandalizing a petrol station, and having a run-in with the police.*

SCRIPT NOTES REGARDING SCENE No. 3 *used to be Duke of New York - Petrol

Station.

The boys have a stolen car.

Alex should have a big bunch of keys.

Smashing windows.

Activity of breaking the car and stealing a car.

Starting a fire in the petrol station.

Two pedestrians run away while they see the gang approaching them

from a far distance already.

Marble Arch tunnel.

Two lady police women.

19 November 1970

52

15 Nov. 1970

GOOD EVENING

GOOD EVENING OFFICER, GOOD EVENING CONSTABLE

MAY I SEE YOUR DRIVING LICENCE AND INSURANCE CERTIFICATE?

CERTAINLY, CONSTABLE. HERE IS THE INSURANCE CERTIFICATE BUT I'M AFRAID

I SEEM TO HAVE LEFT ME LICENCE HOME IN ME OTHER PANTS.

DOES THIS CAR BELONG TO YOU?

NO, SIR. IT BELONGS TO ~~MY FATHER.~~ me ol Dad.

WHAT IS YOUR FATHER'S NAME?

~~SIMPKIN, SIR.~~ Von Dittersdorf

CHRISTIAN NAME?

LEOPOLD.

AND WHAT IS YOUR NAME?

SAME NAME, SIR. SIMPKINS, CHRISTIAN NAME PERCIVAL

WHERE DO YOU LIVE, MR. SIMPKINS

53

Modern Times:
An Interview with Stanley Kubrick

by Philip Strick and Penelope Houston

Published in Sight and Sound, *Spring 1972*

HOW CLOSELY DID YOU WORK WITH ANTHONY BURGESS IN ADAPTING A CLOCKWORK ORANGE FOR THE SCREEN?

I had virtually no opportunity of discussing the novel with Anthony Burgess. He phoned me one evening when he was passing through London and we had a brief conversation on the telephone. It was mostly an exchange of pleasantries. On the other hand, I wasn't particularly concerned about this because in a book as brilliantly written as *A Clockwork Orange* one would have to be lazy not to be able to find the answers to any questions which might arise within the text of the novel itself. I think it is reasonable to say that, whatever Burgess had to say about the story was said in the book.

HOW ABOUT YOUR OWN CONTRIBUTIONS TO THE STORY? YOU SEEM TO HAVE PRESERVED THE STYLE AND STRUCTURE OF THE ORIGINAL FAR MORE CLOSELY THAN WITH MOST OF YOUR PREVIOUS FILMS, AND THE DIALOGUES ARE OFTEN EXACTLY THE SAME AS IN THE NOVEL.

My contribution to the story consisted of writing the screenplay. This was principally a matter of selection and editing, though I did invent a few useful narrative ideas and reshape some of the scenes. However, in general, these contributions merely clarified what was already in the novel—such as the Catlady telephoning the police, which explains why the police appear at the end of that scene. In the novel, it occurs to Alex that she may have called them, but this is the sort of thing that you can do in a novel and not in the screenplay. I was also rather pleased with the idea of "Singin' in the Rain" as a means of Alexander identifying Alex again towards the end of the film.

56

55 Kubrick giving directions to Patrick Magee for the gang rape scene.
56 Kubrick gets a handheld shot of Mrs. Alexander being subjected to atrocities at the hands of Alex and Dim. The painting on the wall is by Kubrick's wife, Christiane, whose work can also be spotted in Eyes Wide Shut.

HOW DID YOU COME TO USE "SINGIN' IN THE RAIN" IN THE FIRST PLACE?

This was one of the more important ideas which arose during rehearsal. This scene, in fact, was rehearsed longer than any other scene in the film and appeared to be going nowhere. We spent three days trying to work out just what was going to happen and somehow it all seemed a bit inadequate. Then the idea popped into my head—I don't know where it came from or what triggered it off.

THE MAIN ADDITION YOU SEEM TO HAVE MADE TO THE ORIGINAL STORY IS THE SCENE OF ALEX'S INTRODUCTION TO THE PRISON. WHY DID YOU FEEL THIS WAS IMPORTANT?

It may be the longest scene but I would not think it is the most important. It was a necessary addition because the prison sequence is compressed, in comparison with the novel, and one had to have something in it which gave sufficient weight to the idea that Alex was actually imprisoned. The routine of checking into prison which, in fact, is quite accurately presented in the film, seemed to provide this necessary weight.

IN THE BOOK THERE IS ANOTHER KILLING BY ALEX WHILE HE IS IN PRISON. BY OMITTING THIS, DON'T YOU RUN THE RISK OF SEEMING TO SHARE ALEX'S OWN OPINION OF HIMSELF AS A HIGH-SPIRITED INNOCENT?

I shouldn't think so, and Alex doesn't see himself as a high-spirited innocent. He is totally aware of his own evil and accepts it with complete openness.

ALEX SEEMS A FAR PLEASANTER PERSON IN THE FILM THAN IN THE BOOK....

Alex makes no attempt to deceive himself or the audience as to his total corruption and wickedness. He is the very personification of evil. On the other hand, he has winning qualities: his total candor, his wit, his intelligence and his energy; these are attractive qualities and ones, I might add, which he shares with Richard III.

66 — Interview by Strick and Houston

Scene 10   Page 2   2.16.70

> Her voice is
> young and
> frightened.
>
> From inside
> the sound
> of clack calck
> clacky clack
> clack clackity
> clackclack of
> someone
> typing, ~~stops.~~ *stops.*
>
> ~~The typing stops.~~

Mr. Alexander: What is it, dear?

Alex: Well, could/~~of~~ *you* your goodness please let him have a cup of water? It's like a faint , you see. It seems as though he's past out in sort of a fainting fit.

Mrs. Alexander: ~~Waitx~~ It's a young man at the door ~~xhexe friendxisxinjured~~ Who says his friend is injured *out on the road.*

Mr. Alexander: Well, for God's sake let him in.

> ~~X~~ The rest of
> the gang, *standing out of sight*
> ~~have~~ slipped
> on rubber
> masks ~~carrying~~
> ~~the impression~~
> of ~~past~~ celebrities:
> Elvis Presley,
> ~~Candixxxhandx~~
> Gahndmi, (sp?)
> Churchill.
>
> As the door opens
> Alex slips on ~~a~~ *Beethoven*
> ~~x~~ mask.
>
> ~~As the door opens~~
> ~~they four~~
> go ~~xuxkingxix~~ roamring
> in. Dim/ jumping
> up and down and
> singing out
> dirty words.
>
> ~~It is a nicely~~
> ~~decorated house.~~
>
> Mrs. Alexander ~~is~~
> ~~about~~ 25 ~~and~~
> very ~~attractive.~~ *cute,*
> *cowers against the wall.*

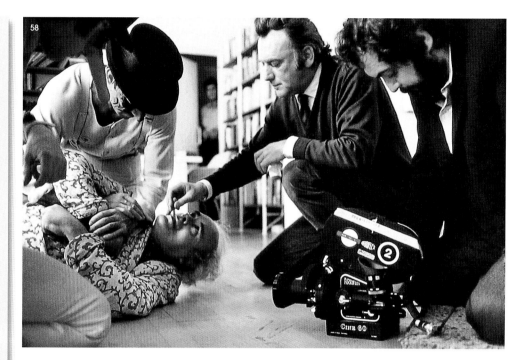

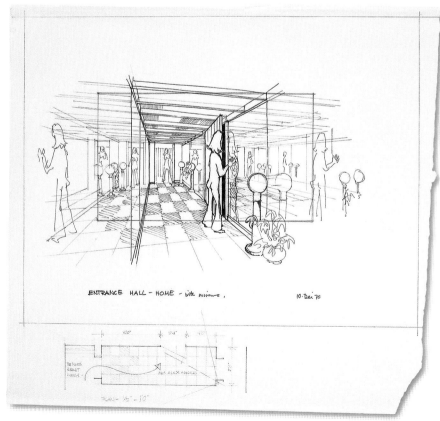

ENTRANCE HALL - HOME - *with mirrors.*   10·Dez 70

57

58

59

60

61

THE VIOLENCE DONE TO ALEX IN THE BRAINWASHING SEQUENCE IS IN FACT MORE HORRIFYING THAN ANYTHING HE DOES HIMSELF....

It was absolutely necessary to give weight to Alex's brutality, otherwise I think there would be moral confusion with respect to what the government does to him. If he were a lesser villain, then one could say: "Oh, yes, of course, he should not be given this psychological conditioning; it's all too horrible and he really wasn't that bad after all." On the other hand, when you have shown him committing such atrocious acts, and you still realize the immense evil on the part of the government in turning him into something less than human in order to make him good, then I think the essential moral idea of the book is clear. It is necessary for man to have choice to be good or evil, even if he chooses evil. To deprive him of this choice is to make him something less than human—a clockwork orange.

BUT AREN'T YOU INVITING A SORT OF IDENTIFICATION WITH ALEX?

I think, in addition to the personal qualities I mentioned, there is the basic psychological,

57 *Draft for the scene of Alex's arrival at the Alexander home. The detail of Alex slipping on a Beethoven mask was later dropped.*
58 *Filming a close shot of Mr. Alexander (Patrick Magee) during the droogs' assault.*
59 *John Barry's design for the Alexanders' entrance hall. Except for the bathroom (created under a tent outside the house) and the entrance hall (constructed in an abandoned factory), the interiors of the Alexanders' home were filmed in a house in Radlett, a short distance from Kubrick's home in Abbot's Mead. The house, known as Skybreak, was designed in 1965 by the British architecture firm Team 4.*
60–61 *McDowell and Adrienne Corri (Mrs. Alexander) rehearse with protective padding and share a hug. McDowell later recalled, "Do you know how many sticks and canes were broken [for the rape scene]? The poor prop man, he made balsa wood ones, he made rubber ones, with a piece of metal in the middle that bent when I hit her.... I went through fifty of them. And Stanley was going crazy because he could not believe the prop man couldn't figure out a way to make a practical stick that wouldn't hurt the poor girl Adrienne Corri."*

62

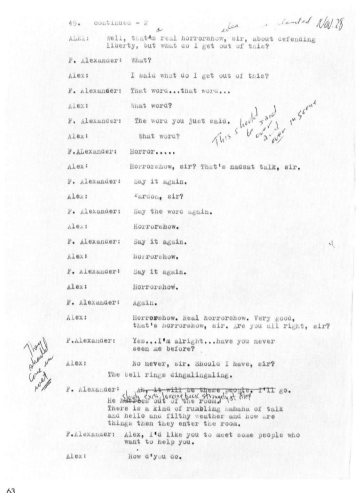

63

the kind of violence that might cause some impulse to emulate it is the "fun" kind of violence: the kind of violence we see in the Bond films or the *Tom and Jerry* cartoons. Unrealistic violence, sanitized violence, violence presented as a joke. This is the only kind of violence that could conceivably cause anyone to wish to copy it, but I am quite convinced that not even this has any effect. There may even be an argument in support of saying that any kind of violence in films, in fact, serves a useful social purpose by allowing people a means of vicariously freeing themselves from the pent up, aggressive emotions which are better expressed in dreams, or in the dreamlike state of watching a film, than in any form of reality of sublimation.

ISN'T THE ASSUMPTION OF YOUR AUDIENCE IN THE CASE OF *A CLOCKWORK ORANGE* LIKELY TO BE THAT YOU SUPPORT ALEX'S POINT OF VIEW AND IN SOME WAY ASSUME RESPONSIBILITY FOR IT?

I don't think that any work of art has a responsibility to be anything but a work of art. There obviously is a considerable controversy, just as there always has been, about what is a work of art, and I should be the last to try to define that. I was amused by Cocteau's *Orphée* when the poet is given the advice: "Astonish me." The Johnsonian definition of a work of art is also meaningful to me, and that is that a work of art must either make life more enjoyable or more endurable. Another quality, which I think forms part of the definition, is that a work of art is always exhilarating and never depressing, whatever its subject matter may be.

IN VIEW OF THE PARTICULAR EXHILARATION OF ALEX'S RELIGIOUS FANTASIES, HAS THE FILM RUN INTO TROUBLE WITH CLERICAL CRITICS?

The reaction of the religious press has been mixed, although a number of superb reviews have been written. One of the most perceptive reviews by the religious press, or any other press, appeared in *The Catholic News* written by John E. Fitzgerald, and I would like to

unconscious identification with Alex. If you look at the story not on the social and moral level, but on the psychological dream content level, you can regard Alex as a creature of the id. He is within all of us. In most cases, this recognition seems to bring a kind of empathy from the audience, but it makes some people very angry and uncomfortable. They are unable to accept this view of themselves and, therefore, they become angry at the film. It's a bit like the king who kills the messenger who brings him bad news and rewards the one who brings him good news.

THE COMPARISON WITH RICHARD III MAKES A STRIKING DEFENSE AGAINST ACCUSATIONS THAT

THE FILM ENCOURAGES VIOLENCE, DELINQUENCY AND SO ON. BUT AS RICHARD IS A SAFELY DISTANT HISTORICAL FIGURE, DOES IT MEET THEM (*SIC*) COMPLETELY?

There is no positive evidence that violence in films or television causes social violence. To focus one's interest on this aspect of violence is to ignore the principal causes, which I would list as:

1. Original sin: the religious view.
2. Unjust economic exploitation: the Marxist view.
3. Emotional and psychological frustration: the psychological view.
4. Genetic factors based on the "Y" chromosome theory: the biological view.
5. Man—the killer ape: the evolutionary view.

To try to fasten any responsibility on art as the cause of life seems to me to have the case put the wrong way around. Art consists of reshaping life but it does not create life, or cause life. Furthermore to attribute powerful suggestive qualities to a film is at odds with the scientifically accepted view that, even after deep hypnosis, in a post-hypnotic state, people cannot be made to do things which are at odds with their natures.

IS THERE ANY KIND OF VIOLENCE IN FILMS WHICH YOU MIGHT REGARD AS SOCIALLY DANGEROUS?

Well, I don't accept that there is a connection, but let us hypothetically say that there might be one. If there were one, I should say that

62 *In an ironic twist of fate, a bloodied and beaten Alex winds up back at the Alexanders' home, but rather than the wife, who has died, it is Mr. Alexander's helper who opens the door.*
63 *In this draft, Mr. Alexander recognizes his assailant by his peculiar vocabulary: the word "horrorshow." It was during shooting that the* idea came to have Mr. Alexander's memory triggered by the song "Singin' in the Rain" instead.*
64 *David Prowse (Julian) and Patrick Magee (Mr. Alexander) wait as assistants style McDowell's hair to look as if he's come in from the rain.*

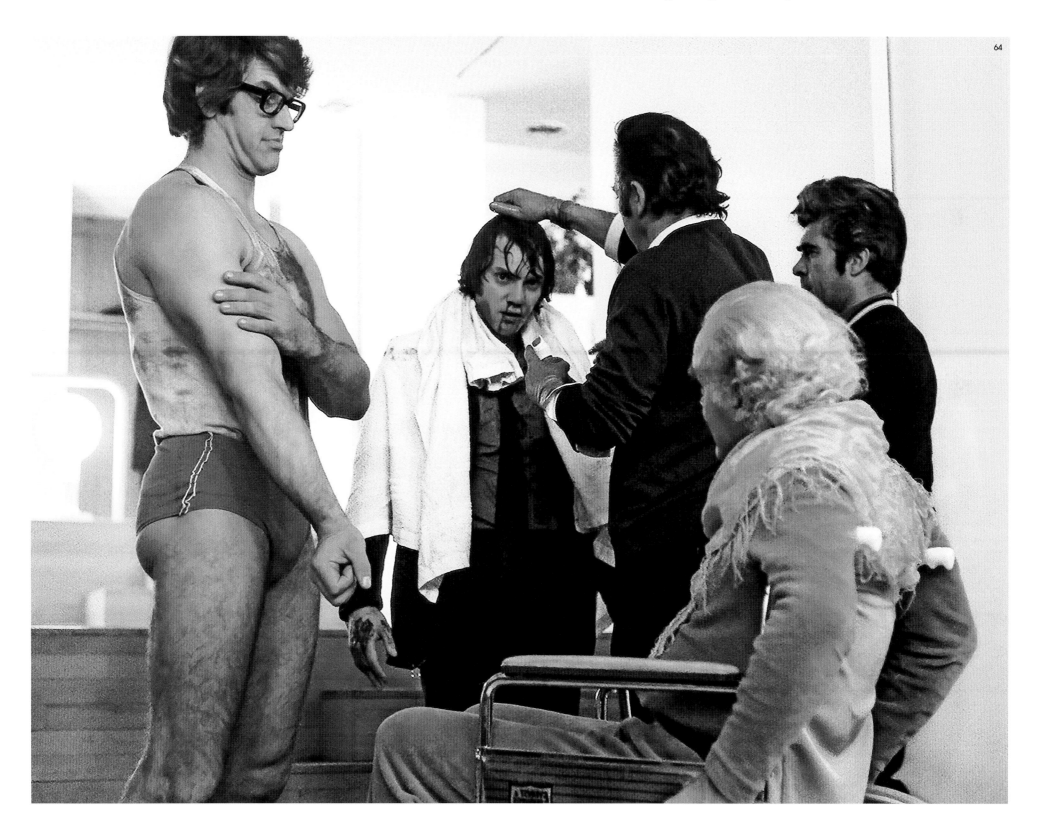

64

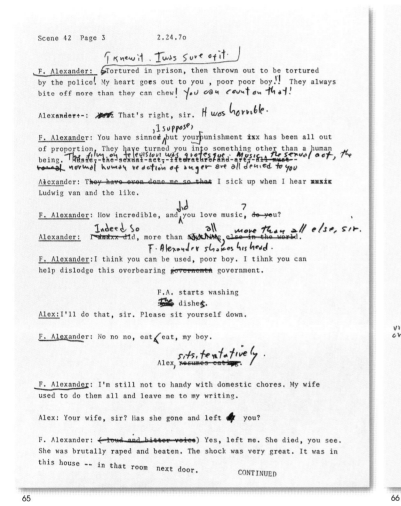

quote one portion of it: "In print we've been told (in B. F. Skinner's *Beyond Freedom and Dignity*) that man is but a grab-bag of conditioned reflexes. On screen with images rather than words, Stanley Kubrick shows that man is more than a mere product of heredity and/or environment. For as Alex's clergyman friend (a character who starts out as a fire-and-brimstone-spouting buffoon but ends up the spokesman for the film's thesis) says: 'When a man cannot choose, he ceases to be a man.'

"The film seems to say that to take away a man's choice is not to redeem but merely to restrain him: otherwise we have a society of oranges, organic but operating like clockwork. Such brainwashing, organic and

psychological, is a weapon that totalitarians in state, church, or society might wish for an easier good even at the cost of individual rights and dignity. Redemption is a complicated thing and change must be motivated from within rather than imposed from without if moral values are to be upheld. But Kubrick is an artist rather than a moralist and he leaves it to us to figure what's wrong and why, what should be done and how it should be accomplished."

YOUR CHOICE OF LENSES FOR THE SHOOTING OF THE FILM OFTEN GIVES IT A SUBTLY DISTORTED VISUAL QUALITY. WHY DID YOU WANT THAT PARTICULAR LOOK?

It may sound like an extremely obvious thing to say, but I think it is worth saying nevertheless that when you are making a film, in addition to any higher purpose you may have in mind, you must be interesting; visually interesting, narratively interesting, interesting from an acting point of view. All ideas for creating interest must be held up against the yardstick of the theme of the story, the narrative requirements and the purpose of the scene; but, within that, you must make a work of art interesting. I recall a comment recorded in a book called *Stanislavski Directs*, in which Stanislavski told an actor that he had the right understanding of the character, the right understanding of the text of the play, that what he was doing

was completely believable, but that it was still no good because it wasn't interesting.

WERE YOU LOOKING AFTER THE HAND-HELD CAMERA FOR THE FIGHT WITH THE CATLADY?

Yes, all of the hand-held camerawork is mine. In addition to the fun of doing the shooting myself, I find it is virtually impossible to explain what you want in a hand-held shot to even the most talented and sensitive camera operator.

TO WHAT EXTENT DO YOU RATIONALIZE A SHOT BEFORE SETTING IT UP?

There are certain aspects of a film which can meaningfully be talked about, but photography and editing do not lend themselves to verbal analysis. It's very much the same as the problem one has talking about painting, or music. The questions of taste involved and the decision-making criteria are essentially nonverbal, and whatever you say about them tends to read like the back of a record album. These are decisions that have to be made every few minutes during the shooting, and they are just down to the director's taste and imagination.

HOW DID YOU COME TO CHOOSE THE PURCELL PIECE—*MUSIC FOR THE FUNERAL OF QUEEN MARY*?

Well, this answer is going to sound a lot like the last one. You're in an area where words are not particularly relevant. In thinking about the music for the scene, the Purcell piece occurred to me and, after I listened to it several times in conjunction with the film, there was simply no question about using it.

THE ARRANGEMENTS BY WALTER CARLOS ARE EXTRAORDINARILY EFFECTIVE....

I think that Walter Carlos has done something completely unique in the field of electronic realization of music—that's the phrase that they use. I think that I've heard most of the

65–67 Script drafts for and shooting of the dinner scene in which Mr. Alexander reveals that his wife died as a result of the assault.

68

THE LESSER CHARACTERS MAY APPEAR RATHER ONE-DIMENSIONAL? THE DANGER OF EVERYTHING THAT YOU DO IN A FILM IS THAT IT MAY NOT WORK, IT MAY BE BORING, OR BLAND, OR STUPID....
When you think of the greatest moments of film, I think you are almost always involved with images rather than scenes, and certainly never dialogue. The thing a film does best is to use pictures with music, and I think these are the moments you remember. Another thing is the way an actor did something: the way Emil Jannings took out his handkerchief and blew his nose in *The Blue Angel,* or those marvelous slow turns that Nikolai Cherkassov did in *Ivan the Terrible.*

HOW DID YOU MANAGE THE SUBJECTIVE SHOT OF ALEX'S SUICIDE ATTEMPT?
We bought an old Newman Sinclair clockwork mechanism camera (no pun intended) for fifty pounds. It's a beautiful camera and it's built like a battleship. We made a number of polystyrene boxes which gave about eighteen inches of protection around the camera, and cut out a slice for the lens. We then threw the camera off a roof. In order to get it to land lens first, we had to do this six times and the camera survived all six drops. On the final one, it landed right on the lens and smashed it but it didn't do a bit of harm to the camera. This, despite the fact that the polystyrene was literally blasted away from it each time by the impact. The next day we shot a steady test on the camera and found there wasn't a thing wrong with it. On this basis, I would say that the Newman Sinclair must be the most indestructible camera ever made.

HOW MUCH PLANNING DO YOU DO BEFORE YOU START TO SHOOT A SCENE?
As much as there are hours in the day, and days in the weeks. I think about a film almost continuously. I try to visualize it and I try to work out every conceivable variation of ideas which might exist with respect to the various scenes, but I have found that when you finally come down to the day the scene is going to be shot and you arrive on the location with

electronic and *musique concrète* LPs there are for sale in Britain, Germany, France, Italy, and the United States; not because I particularly like this kind of music, but out of my researches for *2001* and *Clockwork Orange.* I think Walter Carlos is the only electronic composer and realizer who has managed to create a sound which is not an attempt at copying the instruments of the orchestra and yet which, at the same time, achieves a beauty of its own employing electronic tonalities. I think that his version of the fourth movement of Beethoven's Ninth Symphony rivals hearing a full orchestra playing it, and that is saying an awful lot.

THERE IS VERY LITTLE POST-SYNCHRONIZATION FOR THE DIALOGUE....
There is no post-synchronization. I'm quite pleased about this because every scene was shot on location; even the so-called sets that we built which were, in fact, built in a factory about forty feet off the noisy High Street in Borehamwood, a few hundred yards from the old MGM Studio. Despite this, we were able to get quite acceptably clean soundtracks.

With the modern equipment that's available today in the form of microphones, radio transmitters and so forth, it should be possible to get a usable soundtrack almost anywhere.

In the scene where the tramp recognizes Alex who is standing looking at the Thames, next to the Albert Bridge, there was so much traffic noise on the location that you had to shout in order to be heard, but we were able to get such a quiet soundtrack that it was necessary to add street noise in the final mix to make it realistic. We used a microphone the size of a paper clip, and it was secured with black tape on the tramp's scarf. In several shots you can see the microphone, but you don't know what you are looking at.

IN CONCENTRATING ON THE ACTION OF THE FILM, AS YOU DO, ISN'T THERE A DANGER THAT

the actors, having had the experience of already seeing some scenes shot, somehow it's always different. You find out that you have not really explored the scene to its fullest extent. You may have been thinking about it incorrectly, or you may simply not have discovered one of the variations which now in context with everything else that you have shot is simply better than anything you had previously thought of. The reality of the final moment, just before shooting, is so powerful that all previous analysis must yield before the impressions you receive under these circumstances, and unless you use this feedback to your positive advantage, unless you adjust to it, adapt to it and accept the sometimes terrifying weaknesses it can expose, you can never realize the most out of your film.

HOW DO YOU USUALLY WORK WHEN YOU GET TO THE REALITY OF THE FINAL MOMENT?

Whenever I start a new scene, the most important thing in my mind is, within the needs of the theme and the scene, to make something happen worth putting on film. The most crucial part of this comes when you start rehearsals on a new scene. You arrive on the location, the crew is standing around eating buns and drinking tea, waiting to be told what to do. You've got to keep them outside the room you're rehearsing in and take whatever time is necessary to get everything right, and have it make sense. There's no way to define what this process consists of. It obviously has to do with taste and imagination and it is in this crucial period of time that a film is really created. Once you know you've got something worthwhile, the shooting becomes a matter of recording (improving if you can) what you have already done in rehearsal. Whatever problems exist during the actual shooting are not the kind of problems that worry me. If the actor isn't getting it right, well, he'll get it right eventually. If the

68 *To show Alex's suicide attempt from below, Kubrick shot from beneath a scaffold as a dummy was thrown from the window.*
69 *Kubrick tweaks the lighting.*

"One of the most dangerous fallacies which has influenced a great deal of political and philosophical thinking is that man is essentially good, and that it is society which makes him bad. Rousseau transferred original sin from man to society, and this view has importantly contributed to what I believe has become a crucially incorrect premise on which to base moral and political philosophy."

—SK/1972 (to Bernard Weintraub)

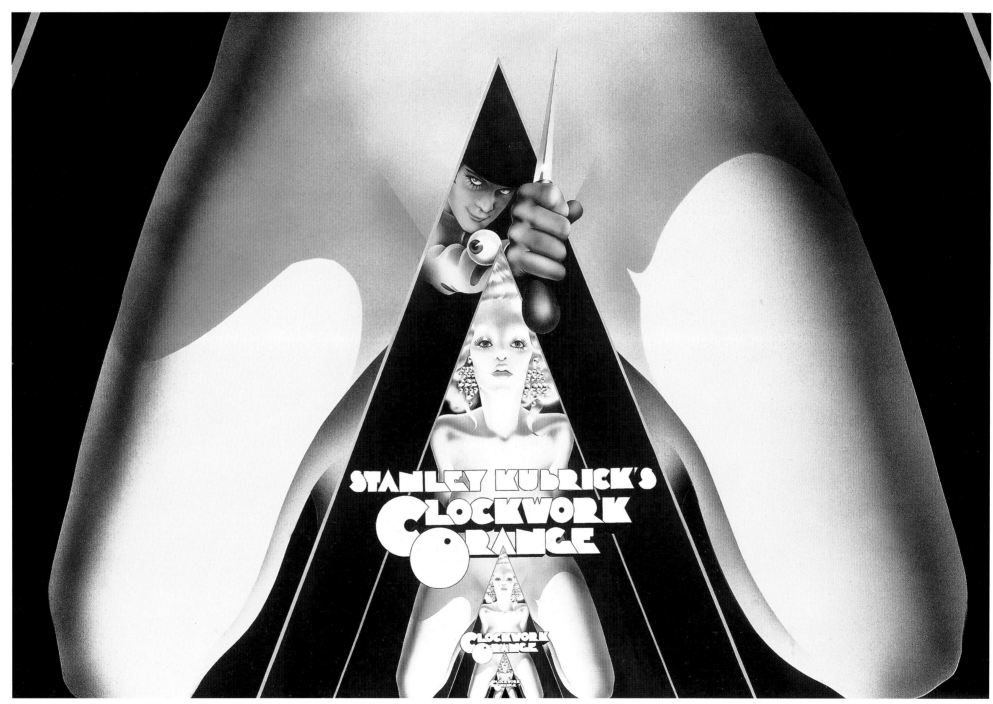

70

70–72 *Philip Castle's poster artwork.*
A variation of 70 was the most common
poster illustration, and 72 was used for
some re-release posters.

camera operator spoils a shot, it can be done again. The thing that can never be changed, and the thing that is the make or break of a picture, are those few hours you spend alone in the actual place with the actors, with the crew outside drinking their tea.

Sometimes you find that the scene is absolutely no good at all. It doesn't make sense when you see it acted. It doesn't provide the necessary emotional or factual information in an interesting way, or in a way which has the right weight to it. Any number of things can suddenly put you in a position where you've got nothing to shoot. The only thing you can say about a moment like this is that it's better to realize it while you still have a chance to change it and to create something new, than it is to record forever something that is wrong. This is the best and the worst time: it is the time you have your most imaginative ideas, things that have not occurred to you before, regardless of how much you've thought about the scene. It's also the time when you can stand there and feel very dumb and unhappy with what you're seeing, and not have the faintest idea of what to do about it.

DO YOU VERY CONSCIOUSLY FAVOR A PARTICULAR STYLE OF SHOOTING?

If something is really happening on the screen, it isn't crucial how it's shot. Chaplin had such a simple cinematic style that it was almost like *I Love Lucy*, but you were always hypnotized by what was going on, unaware of the essentially non-cinematic style. He frequently used cheap sets, routine lighting and so forth, but he made great films. His films will probably last longer than anyone else's. You could say that Chaplin was no style and all content. On the other hand, the opposite can be seen in Eisenstein's films, who is all style and no content or, depending on how generous you want to be, little content. Many of Eisenstein's films are really quite silly; but they are so beautifully made, so brilliantly cinematic, that, despite their heavily propagandistic simplemindedness, they become important.

71

72

Obviously, if you can combine style and content, you have the best of all possible films.

DO YOU HAVE A PREFERENCE FOR ANY ONE ASPECT OF THE WHOLE FILMMAKING PROCESS?

I think I enjoy editing the most. It's the nearest thing to some reasonable environment in which to do creative work. Writing, of course, is very satisfying, but, of course, you're not working with film. The actual shooting of a film is probably the worst circumstances you could try to imagine for creating a work of art. There is, first of all, the problem of getting up very early every morning and going to bed very late every

night. Then there is the chaos, confusion and frequently physical discomfort. It would be, I suppose, like a writer trying to write a book while working at a factory lathe in temperatures which range from 95 to negative 10 degrees Fahrenheit. In addition to this, of course, editing is the only aspect of the cinematic art that is unique. It shares no connection with any other art form: writing, acting, photography, things that are major aspects of the cinema, are still not unique to it, but editing is.

HOW LONG DID THE EDITING TAKE ON *CLOCKWORK ORANGE?*

The editing up to the point of dubbing took about six months, working seven days a week.

DO YOU EVER HAVE PROBLEMS CUTTING OUT YOUR OWN MATERIAL?

When I'm editing, I'm only concerned with the questions of "Is it good or bad?" "Is it necessary?" "Can I get rid of it?" "Does it work?" My identity changes to that of an editor. I am never concerned with how much difficulty there was to shoot something, how much it cost and so forth. I look at the material with completely different eyes. I'm never troubled losing material. I

73

74

75

cut everything to the bone. When you're shooting, you want to make sure that you don't miss anything and you cover it as fully as time and budget allow. When you're editing, you want to get rid of everything that isn't essential.

HOW MUCH SUPPORT COVERAGE DO YOU SHOOT?

There's always a conflict between time, money, and quality. If you shoot a lot of coverage, then you must either spend a lot of money, or settle for less quality of performance. I find that when I'm shooting a scene where the acting is primarily important, I shoot a lot of takes but I don't try to get a lot of coverage from other angles. I try to

shoot the scene as simply as possible to get the maximum performance from the actors without presenting them with the problem of repeating the performance too many times from different angles. On the other hand, in an action scene, where it's relatively easy to shoot, you want lots and lots of angles so that you can do something interesting with it in the cutting room.

DO YOU DIRECT ACTORS IN EVERY DETAIL, OR DO YOU EXPECT THEM TO SOME EXTENT TO COME UP WITH THEIR OWN IDEAS?

I come up with the ideas. That is essentially the director's job. There is a misconception, I think, about what directing actors means: it generally goes along the lines of the direc-

tor imposing his will over difficult actors, or teaching people who don't know how to act. I try to hire the best actors in the world. The problem is comparable to one a conductor might face. There's little joy in trying to get a magnificent performance from a student orchestra. It's difficult enough to get one with all the subtleties and nuances you might want out of the greatest orchestra in the world. You want to have great virtuoso soloists, and so with actors. Then it's not necessary to teach them how to act or to discipline them or to impose your will upon them because there is usually no problem along those lines. An actor will almost always do what you want him to do if he is able to do it; and, therefore, since great actors are able

to do almost anything, you find you have few problems. You can then concentrate on what you want them to do, what is the psychology of the character, what is the purpose of the scene, what is the story about? These are things that are often muddled up and require simplicity and exactitude. The director's job is to provide the actor with ideas, not to teach him how to act or to trick him into acting. There's no way to give an actor what he hasn't got in the form of

73-75 *Airbrush artwork by Philip Castle.*
76 *The film made bold use of sexually explicit imagery, including the nude mannequins that dispense milk from their nipples and this ceramic phallus (made by Dutch artist Herman Makkink in 1969) that Alex uses to attack the Catlady.*

"Alex's adventures are a kind of psychological myth. Our subconscious finds release in Alex, just as it finds release in dreams."
—SK/1971 (to Penelope Houston)

"The essential moral of the story hinges on the question of choice, and the question of whether man can be good without having the choice to be evil, and whether a creature who no longer has this choice is still a man."

—SK/1972 (to Gene Siskel)

77–79 ***Airbrush artwork by Philip Castle.***

talent. You can give him ideas, thoughts, attitudes. The actor's job is to create emotion. Obviously, the actor may have some ideas too, but this is not what his primary responsibility is. You can make a mediocre actor less mediocre, you can make a terrible actor mediocre, but you cannot go very far without the magic. Great performances come from the magical talent of the actor, plus the ideas of the director.

The other part of the director's job is to exercise taste: he must decide whether what he is seeing is interesting, whether it's appropriate, whether it is of sufficient weight, whether it's credible. These are decisions that no one else can make.

YOU MADE WHAT MIGHT SEEM SOME UNUSUAL CASTING CHOICES FOR YOUR LAST TWO FILMS—HOW DO YOU FIND THE ACTORS YOU WANT?

Well, that really comes down to a question of taste, doesn't it? A lot of pictures are cast by producers and their decisions are frequently based on proven success rather than unproven hints at talent. Many producers aren't willing to decide whether an actor who is unknown and who has done very little work is really good. I have nothing against people of proven talent, but sometimes there may be no one in that category who is right for the part.

DO YOU ENJOY WORKING WITH DIFFERENT ACTORS? WITH A FEW EXCEPTIONS—PETER SELLERS, FOR INSTANCE—YOU HAVEN'T OFTEN USED THE SAME ACTOR TWICE, UNLIKE A LOT OF DIRECTORS WHO OBVIOUSLY PREFER TO BUILD UP A SORT OF STOCK COMPANY OF PEOPLE WHO KNOW THEIR WORK.

I don't really think in those terms. I try to choose the best actors for the parts, whether I know them or not. I would avoid actors who have reputations for being destructive and neurotic but, other than that, there is no one whom I would not consider using for a part.

The only thing that is really important in your relationship with actors is that they must know that you admire them, that you admire their work, and there's no way to fake that. You must really admire them or you shouldn't use them. If they know that you admire their work, which they can sense in a thousand different ways, it doesn't really matter what you think of each other or what you say to them, or whether you are terribly friendly or not. The thing they care about is their work. Some actors are very amusing and pleasant and always cheerful. They are, of course, more pleasant to have around than those who are morose, vacant, or enigmatic. But how they behave when you're not shooting has very little to do with what happens when the camera turns over.

YOU MADE *CLOCKWORK ORANGE* INITIALLY BECAUSE YOU HAD TO POSTPONE YOUR NAPOLEON PROJECT. HOW DO YOU SEE THE NAPOLEON FILM DEVELOPING?

First of all, I start from the premise that there has never been a great historical film, and I say that with all apologies and respect to those who have made historical films, including myself. I don't think anyone has ever successfully solved the problem of dealing in an interesting way with the historical information that has to be conveyed, and at the same time getting a sense of reality about the daily life of the characters. You have to get a feeling of what it was like to be with Napoleon. At the same time, you have to convey enough historical information in an intelligent, interesting, and concise way so that the audience understands what happened.

WOULD YOU INCLUDE ABEL GANCE'S *NAPOLEON* IN THIS VERDICT?

I think I would have to. I know that the film is a masterpiece of cinematic invention and it brought cinematic innovations to the screen which are still being called innovations whenever someone is bold enough to try them again. But on the other hand, as a film about Napoleon, I have to say I've always been disappointed in it.

DID YOU THINK OF *CLOCKWORK ORANGE* AS BEING IN ANY WAY A FORM OF RELAXATION BETWEEN TWO VERY BIG FILMS?

I don't think in terms of big movies, or small movies. Each movie presents problems of its own and has advantages of its own. Each movie requires everything that you have to give it, in order to overcome the artistic and logistic problems that it poses. There are advantages in an epic film, just as there are disadvantages. It is much easier to do a huge crowd scene and make it interesting than it is to film a man sitting at a table thinking.

80 *Alex's parents Em (Sheila Raynor) and Pee (Philip Stone) in a cut scene.*
81 *The director claps the clapboard to mark the start of a take.*

A Clockwork Utopia

by Andrew Bailey

The following are excerpts from an interview originally published in Rolling Stone *on January 20, 1972.*

Kubrick doesn't really like talking in a retrospective, analytic way. He likes to freewheel from one topic to another—from the printing costs of newspapers to the defensive style of English soccer.

Kubrick has built around him an organization of machines and people that both protects him ("If somebody from Hollywood wants to see Stanley," says one of his staff, "then the mountain comes to Mohammed") and gives him nearly total freedom within his immediate environment. In short, he sees who he wants to see, when he wants to see them, but it's all done so politely and diplomatically that you don't really mind. He's something like a magnet, the power being hidden behind a rather bland and precise manner. People around him tend to align themselves in his force field.

He can't understand directors who feel the need for holidays after completing a film, even if it took two years to make. "Making films is fun, let's get that straight. Right now I want to start making another one."

Kubrick notices the tape recorder being switched on as he explains his attitude towards the business side of filmmaking. "I can't think of a better way of killing anybody," he says, "than by printing exactly what they say—unless of course they are a naturally colorful character, and I'm certainly not that.

"There's an enormous difference between being chief engineer and architect. Obviously, there are at least two ways of losing what might be loosely described as artistic integrity—one way is imposed on you by others, and the other by yourself. No one can prevent you from losing it yourself, but on the other hand you can handle the 'inner' job only to lose it by not having actual legal authority over your film. The message came across loud and clear, of how important

legal authority was. Under those conditions people who oppose you can be unhelpful, difficult, unpleasant, uncooperative but they can't make you do anything you don't want.

"Unless a distributor treats a film with utmost contempt, they do at least know how to distribute films. And I can't really see cassettes radically altering the situation. There will almost certainly have to be standardization and I should imagine the cassette mustn't cost more than a few dollars—much less than the prices mentioned in the trade press. Something which is liable to have much more of an impact might be color television with the same resolution and sharpness as we now have on film, possibly even three-dimensional holographic presentations distributed via satellites. This fairly simple technological advance would substitute for the vast international organization, part of whose purpose is to deliver prints to the theater and collect them again and also, of course to collect the money from the exhibitors. With the satellite system collection of the money would be as simple as preparing and paying a telephone bill. This type of technology would change the financing and distribution function to one which could be accomplished by smaller companies with much less funding. It would certainly be in the interest of filmmakers to have a greater number of sources of financing and distribution."

One of Kubrick's undoubted touches of wizardry is the timing of his films. *Dr. Strangelove*, perhaps the most powerfully of all, resonated with the feeling of the times. How much does Kubrick think in terms of packaging a product for a particular market?

"Really I don't think of my films in that way at all. I make the assumption that anything I'm interested in will find a sufficient number of people who are also interested. In any event, the classical mistake made by those whose sole aim is to analyze the market and make profits as predictably as they can, is to believe that subject matter is of itself significant commercial consideration. Nothing is of itself interesting or uninteresting to the movie public. It is the particular film that counts.

"It is, of course, not surprising that the financiers of films have always looked for safety in their investments. This is not an unreasonable objective. The paradox is, of course, that what is generally thought to be safety is almost a guarantee of mediocrity and failure. The best way to optimize a film's commerciality—from a producer's point of view, and this is obvious but seemingly little understood—is to use a director who has had previous commercial success.

"I suppose the instinct that you need is like the problem of what you do in an airplane when you stall. Before you learn to be a pilot the instinct is to pull back on the stick, trying to pull the airplane up. But you later realize that no matter how close you are to the ground the only way to recover is to dive the plane faster and pick up flying speed. Trends have always been something associated with safety in film investment. Very often it is as pathetic a delusion as what happens when the witch doctor waves his hand and a total eclipse of the sun happens to occur at the same moment.

"There will of course never be an entirely safe bet because a film must prove to be something that excites the imagination of the audience and makes them go out and tell their friends to see it. I think the thing that stopped *2001* from sparking off a trend was that no one else would have been able to accomplish the technical parts of the films without the know-how and the budget, and neither element seems to be readily available. *Clockwork Orange* cost less than $2,000,000, which I think is rather small for something which is considered as a major film. Actually, the whole of *Clockwork Orange* was shot on location."

* * *

"I first came across *Clockwork Orange*," says Kubrick, "while I was making *2001*. Terry Southern gave me a copy. But I didn't have time to read it then and it lay on a shelf for two and a half years. It was expensive to

buy because it wasn't owned any more by Anthony Burgess, the author. I bought it off the two gentlemen who get their names on the credits as executive producers. I've never even met them. I suppose they must be credited with having thought it was a good enough book to invest money in—though no one is sure how much they paid.

"And prior to completing the film I'd only spoken to Burgess once, more or less just to say hello. This wasn't because I had no interest in his ideas about the story but because his ideas were already there in the book. Did you know that there is a strange last chapter which only appears in one English edition of the book? In it Alex settles down to a suburban sort of life. Apparently, it represents some sort of compromise between Burgess and his publisher. I think it's completely out of tone with the rest of the book. I wasn't even aware of this chapter until I'd been working on the screenplay for four months. I found it difficult to believe.

"Rather than try to explain why I decided to do the book, one can almost say that it's the kind of book that you'd have to look hard to find a reason why not to do. It has everything: great ideas, a great plot, external action, interesting side characters, and one of the most unique leading characters I've ever encountered in fiction—Alex. The only character comparable to Alex is Richard III, and I think they both work on your imagination in much the same way. They both take the audience into their confidence, they are both completely honest, witty, intelligent and unhypocritical.

"I don't know why somebody else didn't make the film first, although one thing I have noticed is that all the books I've made into films, with the exception of *Lolita*, were long ignored. *Paths of Glory* was published about 30 years before it was filmed. *Red Alert*, on which *Strangelove* was based, had been out for ten years. In that case, though, while I started off to make a truly factual film, I realized that the realism of the situation was so ridiculous that the only way to do it was a comedy.

"I'd say that my intention with *Clockwork Orange* was to be faithful to the novel and to try and see the violence in Alex's point of view, to show that it was great fun for him, the happiest part of his life, that it was like some great action ballet. It was necessary to find a way of stylizing the violence, just as Burgess does by his writing style. The ironic counterpoint of the music was certainly one of the ways of achieving this. All the scenes of violence are very different without the music.

"When you ask is it right for violence to be fun, you must realize that people aren't used to challenging whether certain types of violence are fun. You see it when your Western hero finally shoots all the villains. Heroic violence, in the Hollywood sense, is a great deal like the motivational researchers' problem selling candy. The problem is not to convince people that it's good candy, but to free them from the guilt of eating it. We have seen so many times that the body of a film serves merely as an excuse for motivating a final blood-crazed slaughter by the hero of his enemies, and at the same time to relieve the audience's guilt of enjoying this mayhem.

"Really *Clockwork Orange* operates on two levels. One is the sociological argument—the question of the evil committed by the government in trying to change Alex's nature. It's an interesting level, it serves to provide the structure of the plot, but I don't think that it's actually from this aspect that the story derives its uniqueness and its power. More importantly, Alex represents natural man in the state in which he is born, unlimited, unrepressed. When Alex is given the Ludovico treatment, you can say this symbolizes the neurosis created by the conflict between the strictures imposed by society and our own natures. This is why we feel exhilarated when Alex is 'cured' in the final scene. If you accept the idea that one views a film in a state of 'daydream,' then this symbolic dream–like content becomes a powerful factor in influencing your feelings about the film. Since your dreams can take you into areas which can never be part of your conscious mind, I think a work of art can 'operate' on you in much the same way as a dream does.

"The psychological conditioning technique shown in the film is based on nega-tive conditioning, and that is based on the classical Pavlov experiments. The Russians, for instance, trained dogs to run under Nazi tanks with 20 to 30 pounds of high explosives strapped to their bodies, and connected to proximity fuses. They always fed the dogs under tanks, and eventually the dog built up the conditioned reflex of running under a tank when he was hungry.

"You know the authority on all this is Skinner and his latest works state the premise that human freedom and dignity have become inconsistent with the survival of our civilization. It's a very startling and sinister and not totally refutable contention, and *Clockwork Orange* is very concerned with this sort of idea. I like to believe that Skinner is wrong, and that what is sinister is that this philosophy may serve as an intellectual basis for some sort of scientifically oriented repressive government. On the other hand that is partly relevant to the problems we are facing today.

"We are, after all, confronted with a very paradoxical situation in which we have a highly complex civilization which requires an equally complex social structure and political authority for it to function at all. This set against the ever widening sense that legal and political activity has become a waste of time, and that the goal should be to destroy all authority so that man in all his natural goodness may emerge.

"This Utopian view is a dangerous fallacy. The history of all such efforts shows they eventually fall into the hands of thugs. In addition to this I don't share the view that the weakness we find in human nature primarily stems from an improperly structured society. I find the fault is the very imperfect nature of man himself, who has been described as the missing link between primitive ape and a civilized human being.

"Another area where Skinner should be attacked is in his attempt to formulate a total philosophy of the human personality solely in terms of conditioning. This is a dreary conception. I like to believe that there are cer-tain aspects of the human personality which are essentially unique and mysterious."

Some of the actors used by Kubrick may be surprised by his almost traditional religious view of mankind. When it comes to the business of filmmaking, Kubrick adopts a far more scientific stance. For instance, a computer ("one of man's most beautiful inventions") is sometimes used to work out the most efficient order for scenes to be shot.

"An actor," says Kubrick, "is essentially an emotion-producing machine. His job is to produce authentic emotions. The director's job is to make sure that this emotion is appropriate, meaningful, and interesting. It's equivalent to the novelist deciding which adjective to use. The greatest mistake a director can make is to think of himself as an acting teacher. By the time you get in front of a camera it's too late. The director is the only feedback an actor gets in trying to relate his performance to the eventual audience, therefore the director's views are crucial to the actor. The only important thing in the relationship is that the actor must know you respect him and his work. There isn't a great deal of magic to this side of it."

83 *The Alexanders' home was decorated with futuristic-looking furniture such as this heart-shaped double lounge.*
84 *The Chelsea Drugstore on King's Road in London served as the location for the Music Bootick where Alex picks up two young women. (Note the 2001 LP placed at the front of the bin.)*
85 *Kubrick in a moment of solitary concentration.*

Filmography

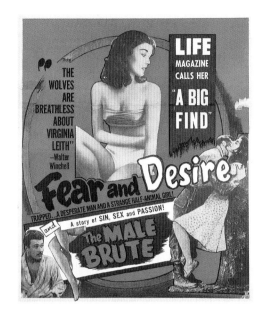

Day of the Fight
1950 / BLACK AND WHITE / 12 MINUTES

PRINCIPAL CAST
HIMSELF WALTER CARTIER
HIMSELF VINCENT CARTIER
HIMSELF NATE FLEISCHER
(BOXING HISTORIAN)
WALTER CARTIER'S OPPONENT
BOBBY JAMES
RINGSIDE FAN JUDY SINGER
MAIN CREDITS
PRODUCED AND DIRECTED BY
STANLEY KUBRICK
SCREENPLAY STANLEY KUBRICK
EDITOR JULIAN BERGMAN
ASSISTANT DIRECTOR ALEXANDER SINGER
NARRATION SCRIPT ROBERT REIN
NARRATOR DOUGLAS EDWARDS
PHOTOGRAPHY STANLEY KUBRICK
ORIGINAL MUSIC GERALD FRIED
SOUND STANLEY KUBRICK
2ND UNIT DIRECTOR, ADDITIONAL
PHOTOGRAPHY ALEXANDER SINGER
(uncredited)
EDITING, SOUND STANLEY KUBRICK
(uncredited)

Flying Padre
1951 / BLACK AND WHITE / 9 MINUTES
Distributed by RKO RADIO

PRODUCED BY BURTON BENJAMIN
DIRECTED BY STANLEY KUBRICK
NARRATOR BOB HITE
EDITOR ISAAC KLEINERMAN
MUSIC NATHANIEL SHILKRET
SCREENPLAY, PHOTOGRAPHY
STANLEY KUBRICK (uncredited)

The Seafarers
1953 / COLOR / 30 MINUTES
Distributed by THE SEAFARERS
INTERNATIONAL UNION / AFI

AS TOLD BY DON HOLLENBECK
WRITTEN BY WILL CHASEN
DIRECTED AND PHOTOGRAPHED BY
STANLEY KUBRICK
PRODUCED BY LESTER COOPER

Fear and Desire
1953 / BLACK AND WHITE / 68 MINUTES
Distributed by JOSEPH BURSTYN INC.

PRINCIPAL CAST
MAC FRANK SILVERA
SIDNEY PAUL MAZURSKY
LT. CORBY & THE GENERAL
KENNETH HARP
FLETCHER & THE CAPTAIN STEVE COIT
MAIN CREDITS
DIRECTED, PHOTOGRAPHED,
AND EDITED BY STANLEY KUBRICK
SCREENPLAY HOWARD SACKLER and
STANLEY KUBRICK
PRODUCED BY STANLEY KUBRICK
ASSOCIATE PRODUCER MARTIN PERVELER
DIALOGUE DIRECTOR TOBA KUBRICK
ART DIRECTION HERBERT LEBOWITZ
ORIGINAL MUSIC GERALD FRIED

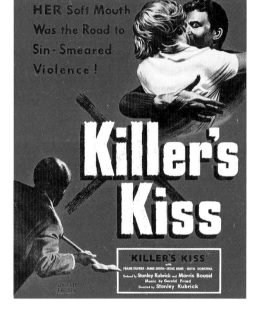

Killer's Kiss
1955 / BLACK AND WHITE / 67 MINUTES
Distributed by UNITED ARTISTS

PRINCIPAL CAST
VINCENT RAPALLO FRANK SILVERA
DAVY GORDON JAMIE SMITH
GLORIA PRICE IRENE KANE
IRIS PRICE RUTH SOBOTKA
MAIN CREDITS
EDITED, PHOTOGRAPHED,
AND DIRECTED BY STANLEY KUBRICK
PRODUCED BY STANLEY KUBRICK
and MORRIS BOUSEL
STORY BY STANLEY KUBRICK
SCREENPLAY HOWARD SACKLER and
STANLEY KUBRICK (uncredited)
ORIGINAL MUSIC GERALD FRIED
PRODUCTION MANAGER IRA MARVIN
CAMERA OPERATORS JESSE PALEY,
MAX GLENN
ASSISTANT EDITORS PAT JAFFE,
ANTHONY BEZICH
ASSISTANT DIRECTOR ERNEST NUKANEN
CHOREOGRAPHY DAVID VAUGHAN

The Killing
1956 / BLACK AND WHITE / 83 MINUTES
Distributed by UNITED ARTISTS

PRINCIPAL CAST
JOHNNY CLAY STERLING HAYDEN
FAY COLEEN GRAY
VAL CANNON VINCE EDWARDS
MAIN CREDITS
DIRECTED BY STANLEY KUBRICK
PRODUCED BY JAMES B. HARRIS
SCREENPLAY STANLEY KUBRICK (based on
Lionel White's novel *Clean Break*)
DIALOGUE JIM THOMPSON
ASSOCIATE PRODUCER
ALEXANDER SINGER
CAMERA OPERATOR DICK TOWER
DIRECTOR OF PHOTOGRAPHY
LUCIEN BALLARD
ART DIRECTOR RUTH SOBOTKA
FILM EDITOR BETTY STEINBERG
ORIGINAL MUSIC GERALD FRIED
SPECIAL EFFECTS DAVE KOEHIER
SET DECORATOR HARRY REIF

Paths of Glory
1957 / BLACK AND WHITE / 87 MINUTES
Distributed by UNITED ARTISTS

PRINCIPAL CAST
COLONEL DAX KIRK DOUGLAS
GENERAL BROULARD ADOLPHE MENJOU
GENERAL MIREAU GEORGE MACREADY
CORPORAL PARIS RALPH MEEKER
LIEUTENANT ROGET WAYNE MORRIS
MAJ. SAINT-AUBAN RICHARD ANDERSON
PRIVATE ARNAUD JOSEPH TURKEL
PRIVATE FERAL TIMOTHY CAREY
GERMAN GIRL CHRISTIANE KUBRICK
(as Susanne Christian)
MAIN CREDITS
DIRECTED BY STANLEY KUBRICK
PRODUCED BY JAMES B. HARRIS
SCREENPLAY STANLEY KUBRICK, CALDER
WILLINGHAM, and JIM THOMPSON
(based on the novel by Humphrey Cobb)
EDITOR EVA KROLL
DIRECTOR OF PHOTOGRAPHY
GEORGE KRAUSE
ORIGINAL MUSIC GERALD FRIED
ART DIRECTOR LUDWIG REIBER

Spartacus
1960 / COLOR / 197 MINUTES
Distributed by UNIVERSAL PICTURES

PRINCIPAL CAST
SPARTACUS KIRK DOUGLAS
CRASSUS LAURENCE OLIVIER
ANTONINUS TONY CURTIS
VARINIA JEAN SIMMONS
GRACCHUS CHARLES LAUGHTON
BATIATUS PETER USTINOV
JULIUS CAESAR JOHN GAVIN
HELENA NINA FOCH
TIGRANES HERBERT LOM
CRIXUS JOHN IRELAND
GLABRUS JOHN DALL
MARCELLUS CHARLES MCGRAW
CLAUDIA JOANNA BARNES
DAVID HAROLD J. STONE
DRABA WOODY STRODE
RAMON PETER BROCCO
MAIN CREDITS
DIRECTED BY STANLEY KUBRICK
EXECUTIVE PRODUCER KIRK DOUGLAS
PRODUCED BY EDWARD LEWIS
SCREENPLAY DALTON TRUMBO (based on
the novel by Howard Fast)
DIRECTOR OF PHOTOGRAPHY
RUSSELL METTY
PRODUCTION DESIGNER
ALEXANDER GOLITZEN
ORIGINAL MUSIC ALEX NORTH
ART DIRECTOR ERIC ORBOM
SET DECORATIONS RUSSELL A. GAUSMAN,
JULIA HERON
EDITOR ROBERT LAWRENCE

Lolita
1962 / BLACK AND WHITE / 153 MINUTES
Distributed by METRO-GOLDWYN-MAYER

PRINCIPAL CAST
HUMBERT HUMBERT JAMES MASON
CLARE QUILTY PETER SELLERS
CHARLOTTE HAZE SHELLEY WINTERS
LOLITA HAZE SUE LYON
DICK GARY COCKRELL
JOHN FARLOW JERRY STOVIN
JEAN FARLOW DIANA DECKER
NURSE MARY LORE LOIS MAXWELL
PHYSICIAN CEC LINDER
MRS. STARCH SHIRLEY DOUGLAS
VIVIAN DARKBLOOM MARIANNE STONE
MAIN CREDITS
DIRECTED BY STANLEY KUBRICK
PRODUCED BY JAMES B. HARRIS
SCREENPLAY VLADIMIR NABOKOV
ORIGINAL MUSIC NELSON RIDDLE
"LOLITA" THEME BOB HARRIS, orchestrations
by GIL GRAU
PRODUCTION SUPERVISOR
RAYMOND ANZARUT
ART DIRECTOR BILL ANDREWS
ASSOCIATE ART DIRECTOR SIDNEY CAIN
DIRECTOR OF PHOTOGRAPHY
OSWALD MORRIS B. S. C.
EDITOR ANTHONY HARVEY
PRODUCTION MANAGER ROBERT STERNE

Dr. Strangelove, or: How I Learned to Stop Worrying and Love the Bomb
1964 / BLACK AND WHITE / 93 MINUTES
Distributed by COLUMBIA PICTURES

PRINCIPAL CAST
**GROUP CAPTAIN LIONEL MANDRAKE,
PRESIDENT MUFFLEY, AND DR.
STRANGELOVE** PETER SELLERS
GENERAL BUCK TURGIDSON
GEORGE C. SCOTT
GENERAL JACK D. RIPPER STERLING HAYDEN
COLONEL BAT GUANO KEENAN WYNN
MAJOR T. J. "KING" KONG SLIM PICKENS
AMBASSADOR DE SADESKY PETER BULL
**LIEUTENANT LOTHAR ZOGG,
BOMBARDIER** JAMES EARL JONES
MISS SCOTT TRACY REED
MR. STAINES JACK CRELEY
LIEUTENANT H. R. DIETRICH, D. S. O.
FRANK BERRY
ADMIRAL RANDOLPH ROBERT O'NEIL
LIEUTENANT W. D. KIVEL, NAVIGATOR
GLENN BECK

MAIN CREDITS
DIRECTED AND PRODUCED BY
STANLEY KUBRICK
SCREENPLAY STANLEY KUBRICK, TERRY
SOUTHERN, and PETER GEORGE (based
on the book *Red Alert* by Peter George)
ART DIRECTOR PETER MURTON
DIRECTOR OF PHOTOGRAPHY
GILBERT TAYLOR
FILM EDITOR ANTHONY HARVEY
PRODUCTION DESIGNER KEN ADAM
SPECIAL EFFECTS WALLY VEEVERS
MAKEUP STUART FREEBORN
MUSIC LAURIE JOHNSON

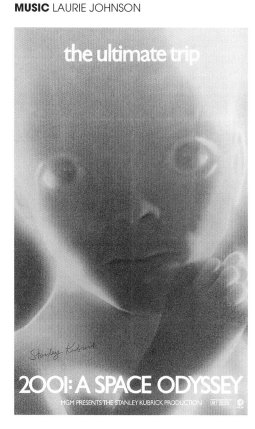

2001: A Space Odyssey
1968 / COLOR / 149 MINUTES
Distributed by METRO-GOLDWYN-MAYER

PRINCIPAL CAST
DAVID BOWMAN KEIR DULLEA
FRANK POOLE GARY LOCKWOOD
DR. HEYWOOD FLOYD WILLIAM SYLVESTER

MOON-WATCHER DANIEL RICHTER
SMYSLOV LEONARD ROSSITER
ELENA MARGARET TYZACK
HALVORSEN ROBERT BEATTY
MICHAELS SEAN SULLIVAN
VOICE OF HAL 9000 DOUGLAS RAIN
MISSION CONTROL FRANK MILLER
POOLE'S FATHER ALAN GIFFORD
POOLE'S MOTHER ANN GILLIS
STEWARDESS PENNY BRAHMS
FLOYD'S DAUGHTER VIVIAN KUBRICK
(uncredited)
MAIN CREDITS
DIRECTED AND PRODUCED BY
STANLEY KUBRICK
SCREENPLAY STANLEY KUBRICK and
ARTHUR C. CLARKE
**SPECIAL PHOTOGRAPHIC EFFECTS
DESIGNED AND DIRECTED BY**
STANLEY KUBRICK
**SPECIAL PHOTOGRAPHIC EFFECTS
SUPERVISORS** WALLY VEEVERS,
DOUGLAS TRUMBULL, CON PEDERSON,
TOM HOWARD
PRODUCTION DESIGNERS TONY MASTERS,
HARRY LANGE, ERNEST ARCHER
FILM EDITOR RAY LOVEJOY
DIRECTOR OF PHOTOGRAPHY
GEOFFREY UNSWORTH
ADDITIONAL PHOTOGRAPHY JOHN ALCOTT
FIRST ASSISTANT DIRECTOR
DEREK CRACKNELL
SPECIAL PHOTOGRAPHIC EFFECTS UNIT
COHN J. CANTWELL, BRYAN LOFTUS,
FREDERICK MARTIN, BRUCE LOGAN,
DAVID OSBORNE, JOHN JACK MALICK
ART DIRECTOR JOHN HOESLI
MAKEUP STUART FREEBORN
SCIENTIFIC CONSULTANT
FREDERICK I. ORDWAY III
ASSISTANTS TO MR. KUBRICK
ANTHONY FREWIN, ANDREW BIRKIN
FRONT PROJECTION SUPERVISOR
TOM HOWARD
"DAWN OF MAN" CHOREOGRAPHY
DANIEL RICHTER
EXPLOITATION DESIGNER, MODEL DESIGNER
CHRISTIANE KUBRICK

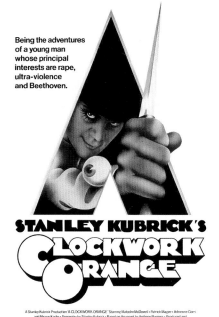

A Clockwork Orange
1971 / COLOR / 137 MINUTES
Distributed by WARNER BROS.

PRINCIPAL CAST
ALEX MALCOLM MCDOWELL
MR. ALEXANDER PATRICK MAGEE
DIM WARREN CLARKE
GEORGIE JAMES MARCUS
DELTOID AUBREY MORRIS
PRISON CHAPLAIN GODFREY QUIGLEY
MINISTER OF THE INTERIOR
ANTHONY SHARP
BILLY BOY RICHARD CONNAUGHT
MRS. ALEXANDER ADRIENNE CORRI
CATLADY MIRIAM KARLIN
MAIN CREDITS
PRODUCED AND DIRECTED BY
STANLEY KUBRICK
SCREENPLAY STANLEY KUBRICK
(based on the novel by Anthony Burgess)
EXECUTIVE PRODUCERS
MAX L. RAAB and SI LITVINOFF
ASSISTANT TO THE PRODUCER JAN HARLAN
LIGHTING CAMERAMAN JOHN ALCOTT
PRODUCTION DESIGNER JOHN BARRY

EDITOR BILL BUTLER
ART DIRECTORS RUSSELL HAGG,
PETER SHEILDS
COSTUME DESIGNER MILENA CANONERO
SPECIAL PAINTINGS AND SCULPTURE
HERMAN MAKKINK, CORNELIUS MAKKINK,
LIZ MOORE, CHRISTIANE KUBRICK
ADDITIONAL PHOTOGRAPHY
STANLEY KUBRICK

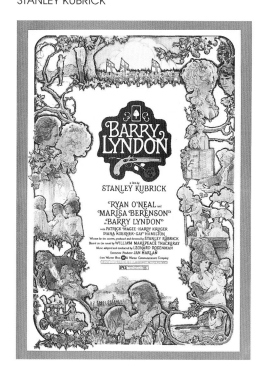

Barry Lyndon
1975 / COLOR / 185 MINUTES
Distributed by WARNER BROS.

PRINCIPAL CAST
BARRY LYNDON RYAN O'NEAL
LADY LYNDON MARISA BERENSON
CHEVALIER DE BALIBARI PATRICK MAGEE
CAPTAIN POTZDORF HARDY KRÜGER
LORD LUDD STEVEN BERKOFF
NORA BRADY GAY HAMILTON
BARRY'S MOTHER MARIE KEAN
GERMAN GIRL DIANA KOERNER
REVEREND RUNT MURRAY MELVIN
LORD WENDOVER ANDRE MORELL
CAPTAIN GROGAN GODFREY QUIGLEY

CAPTAIN QUIN LEONARD ROSSITER
GRAHAM PHILIP STONE
LORD BULLINGDON LEON VITALI
YOUNG BULLINGDON DOMINIC SAVAGE
NARRATOR MICHAEL HORDERN
LORD HALLAM ANTHONY SHARP
MAIN CREDITS
**WRITTEN FOR THE SCREEN, PRODUCED
AND DIRECTED BY** STANLEY KUBRICK
(based on the novel by William Makepeace
Thackeray)
MUSIC ADAPTED AND CONDUCTED BY
LEONARD ROSENMAN
EXECUTIVE PRODUCER JAN HARLAN
PRODUCTION DESIGNER KEN ADAM
DIRECTOR OF PHOTOGRAPHY JOHN ALCOTT
COSTUME DESIGNERS ULLA-BRITT
SØDERLUND, MILENA CANONERO
EDITOR TONY LAWSON
ART DIRECTOR ROY WALKER

The Shining
1980 / COLOR / 145 MINUTES
Distributed by WARNER BROS.

PRINCIPAL CAST
JACK TORRANCE JACK NICHOLSON
WENDY TORRANCE SHELLEY DUVALL
DANNY DANNY LLOYD
HALLORANN SCATMAN CROTHERS
ULLMAN BARRY NELSON
GRADY PHILIP STONE
LLOYD JOE TURKEL
MAIN CREDITS
PRODUCED AND DIRECTED BY
STANLEY KUBRICK
EXECUTIVE PRODUCER JAN HARLAN
SCREENPLAY STANLEY KUBRICK and DIANE
JOHNSON (based on the novel by Stephen King)
DIRECTOR OF PHOTOGRAPHY
JOHN ALCOTT
PRODUCTION DESIGNER ROY WALKER
EDITOR RAY LOVEJOY
COSTUME DESIGNER MILENA CANONERO
STEADICAM OPERATOR GARRETT BROWN
PERSONAL ASSISTANT TO THE DIRECTOR
LEON VITALI

ART DIRECTOR LES TOMKINS
ASSISTANT DIRECTORS TERRY NEEDHAM,
MICHAEL STEVENSON

Full Metal Jacket
1987 / COLOR / 116 MINUTES
Distributed by WARNER BROS.

PRINCIPAL CAST
PVT. JOKER MATTHEW MODINE
ANIMAL MOTHER ADAM BALDWIN
PVT. PYLE VINCENT D'ONOFRIO
GUNNERY SGT. HARTMAN LEE ERMEY
EIGHTBALL DORIAN HAREWOOD
RAFTERMAN KEVYN MAJOR HOWARD
PVT. COWBOY ARLISS HOWARD
LT. TOUCHDOWN ED O'ROSS
LT. LOCKHART JOHN TERRY
DA NANG HOOKER PAPILLON SOO SOO
V. C. SNIPER NGOC LE
MOTORBIKE HOOKER LEANNE HONG
MAIN CREDITS
DIRECTED AND PRODUCED BY
STANLEY KUBRICK

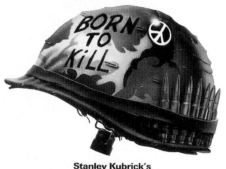

SCREENPLAY STANLEY KUBRICK,
MICHAEL HERR, and GUSTAV HASFORD
(based on the novel *The Short-Timers*
by Gustav Hasford)
EXECUTIVE PRODUCER JAN HARLAN
ASSOCIATE PRODUCER MICHAEL HERR
ASSISTANT TO THE DIRECTOR LEON VITALI
DIRECTOR OF PHOTOGRAPHY
DOUGLAS MILSOME
PRODUCTION DESIGNER ANTON FURST
EDITOR MARTIN HUNTER
COSTUME DESIGNER KEITH DENNY

Eyes Wide Shut
1999 / COLOR / 159 MINUTES
Distributed by WARNER BROS.

PRINCIPAL CAST
DR. WILLIAM HARFORD TOM CRUISE
ALICE HARFORD NICOLE KIDMAN
VICTOR ZIEGLER SYDNEY POLLACK
NICK NIGHTINGALE TODD FIELD
MARION MARIE RICHARDSON
DOMINO VINESSA SHAW

MILICH RADE SHERBEDGIA
DESK CLERK ALAN CUMMING
HELENA HARFORD MADISON EGINTON
MANDY JULIENNE DAVIS
MILICH'S DAUGHTER LEELEE SOBIESKI
MYSTERIOUS WOMAN ABIGAIL GOOD
RED CLOAK LEON VITALI
MAIN CREDITS
PRODUCED AND DIRECTED BY
STANLEY KUBRICK
SCREENPLAY STANLEY KUBRICK and FREDERIC
RAPHAEL (inspired by Arthur Schnitzler's
Traumnovelle)
EXECUTIVE PRODUCER JAN HARLAN
ASSISTANT TO THE DIRECTOR LEON VITALI
DIRECTOR OF PHOTOGRAPHY LARRY SMITH
PRODUCTION DESIGNERS LES TOMKINS,
ROY WALKER
EDITOR NIGEL GALT
COSTUME DESIGNER MARIT ALLEN
ASSISTANT TO STANLEY KUBRICK
ANTHONY FREWIN
CASTING DENISE CHAMIAN, LEON VITALI
1ST ASSISTANT DIRECTOR BRIAN W. COOK

Biography

86

1928
July 26: Stanley Kubrick born in Manhattan to Jacques and Gertrude (Perveler) Kubrick. The family lives in the Bronx.
1934
May 21: Barbara Kubrick, sister, born.
1935
Scores above average on standard reading and intelligence tests.
1940-41
Kubrick spends the fall and spring semesters with uncle, Martin Perveler, in California.
1943
Becomes active in his school's photography club, using his father's Graflex camera.
1945
During his senior year of high school, Kubrick sells his first photograph to *Look* magazine, for $25. It appears in the June 26th issue.
1946
Kubrick graduates from Taft High School, enrolls in evening classes at City College, and becomes a staff photographer for *Look*.
1947
August 15: Kubrick gets his pilot's license.
1948
May 29: Kubrick marries fellow Bronx native Toba Etta Metz (b.1930).

1949
Look publishes "Prizefighter," Kubrick's photo story on middleweight boxer Walter Cartier. Kubrick seeks financing for the script that would eventually become *Fear and Desire*.
1950
Kubrick directs and edits his first film, *Day of the Fight*, a documentary short about boxer Walter Cartier.
1951
Kubrick sells *Day of the Fight* to RKO-Pathé for $4000, the largest sum ever paid by the company for a short.
April 26: *Day of the Fight* opens at the Paramount Theater in New York City.
Directs the short documentary *Flying Padre*, about a priest in rural New Mexico who flies by Piper Cub to visit remote parishioners.
Though his only source of income is money earned playing chess in Washington Square Park, Kubrick resigns from *Look* to pursue a filmmaking career.
Raises nearly $10,000 from friends and family to make *Fear and Desire*. Kubrick edits the picture and soundtrack himself in New York.
1953
March 26: *Fear and Desire* is previewed in New York and praised by *Variety*, then secures a theatrical run at the Guild Theater in New York. Kubrick directs his first film in color, a 16 mm industrial short. *The Seafarers*.
Begins writing his next feature film, *Killer's Kiss*.

87

1954
Raises $40,000 for *Killer's Kiss* and shoots the film on location in New York City.
1955
January: Kubrick divorces Toba Metz and marries ballerina and choreographer Ruth Sobotka (1925–1967).
Edits *Killer's Kiss* and *sells* the film to United Artists for worldwide distribution.
1956
Partners with James B. Harris.
They buy the rights to Lionel White's novel *Clean Break*. The screenplay, titled *The Killing*, is written by Kubrick and novelist Jim Thompson. Shooting takes place at the old Chaplin Studio in Hollywood on sets designed by Ruth Sobotka.
May 20: *The Killing* is released by United Artists.
1957
Harris-Kubrick Pictures signs a deal with MGM president Dore Schary to write, produce, and direct a film for $75,000. Kubrick selects Humphrey Cobb's *Paths of Glory*. After MGM fires Schary and cancels the contract, United Artists agrees to pick up the project.
Kirk Douglas accepts the lead role and the film is shot on location in Munich, Germany.
Kubrick divorces Sobotka and marries Christiane Susanne Harlan (b.1932), the German actress cast for the final scene of *Paths of Glory*, and becomes step-father to Katharina (born in 1953).
Paths of Glory is banned in France, on the Army and Air Force Military circuit in Europe, and Switzerland.
1958
May 12: Kubrick signs on to direct and co-write a film starring Marlon Brando based on a screenplay by Sam Peckinpah.
The two parts ways in November, with Brando taking over as director.
1959
February 13: *Spartacus* star and producer Kirk Douglas fires director Anthony Mann mid-shoot and hires Kubrick to replace him.
April 6: Daughter Anya Renata Kubrick born.
Harris-Kubrick purchases the rights to *Lolita*.
December: Nabokov, after initially refusing

88

due to censorship concerns, agrees to write the screenplay.
1960
August 5: Daughter Vivian Vanessa Kubrick born.
Nabokov completes the script draft, which, though rewritten by Kubrick, is credited only to Nabokov.
Harris-Kubrick turns down a Warner Bros. deal that doesn't give Kubrick complete control.
October 19: *Spartacus* premieres at the Pantages Theater in Hollywood.
1961
Harris makes a deal with Associated Artists for $1,000,000.
James Mason agrees to play Humbert Humbert.
Harris-Kubrick decides to make *Lolita* in England under the Eady plan, which allowed write offs to foreign producers. It is filmed at Elstree Studios, on the outskirts of London.
After negotiations and re-cutting, *Lolita* is given a code seal.
1962
June 13: After battles with censors and the Catholic Church, *Lolita* opens in New York.
Kubrick's Polaris Productions buys the rights to *Red Alert* by Peter George for $3,500.
Harris-Kubrick Pictures is amicably dissolved when Harris decides to pursue a directorial career.
Kubrick and George begin work on a serious adaptation of *Red Alert*; Kubrick later decides to make a comedic satire and hires Terry Southern to co-write.

86 **Ten-year-old Stanley is seen holding his camera in this photograph taken by his father at a local airfield.**
87 **Posing for a publicity shot, late 1950s/early 1960s.**
88 **Playing chess at the set of Dr. Strangelove, 1963.**
89 **Christiane and Stanley Kubrick, ca. 1959.**
90 **A Clockwork Orange was featured on the cover of the British film journal Sight and Sound.**

With Peter Sellers playing three roles and Ken Adam as production designer, *Dr. Strangelove* is produced at Shepperton Studios in England.

1964

Dr. Strangelove, or: How I Learned to Stop Worrying and Love the Bomb is released.

Kubrick writes to Arthur C. Clarke about making a "'really good' science-fiction movie."

Spring: the two meet for up to ten hours a day discussing ideas for the project.

May 20: Clarke signs a formal contract with Kubrick that includes the sale of "The Sentinel" as well as six other short stories.

December 25: Clarke finishes first draft of the novel that will be the basis of the script.

1965

Kubrick sells the project, whose working title is "Journey Beyond the Stars," to MGM and Cinerama.

Kubrick conducts research on the subjects of space, science, and religion, and assembles the special-effects team.

December 29: principal photography begins on *2001: A Space Odyssey* and will last two years

1968

March: shooting wraps up and Kubrick edits the film in New York.

After screening the film for MGM executives, Kubrick deletes a prologue of experts discussing the possible existence of extraterrestrials and a voice-over narration.

April 3: *2001: A Space Odyssey* opens in New York City. Two days later, Kubrick cuts 19 minutes from the original version.

1969

Kubrick and his family move to Abbot's Mead, in England.

Kubrick wins Academy Award for Best Special Visual Effects for *2001: A Space Odyssey*.

Pre-production begins for "Napoleon."

1970

United Artists agrees to produce "Napoleon" but then backs out.

Kubrick considers adapting Arthur Schnitzler's *Traumnovelle* instead (this project would eventually become *Eyes Wide Shut*).

Kubrick secures the rights to Anthony Burgess's novel *A Clockwork Orange*, and Warner Bros. signs the project.

May 15: Kubrick completes first draft of the adaptation of *A Clockwork Orange*.

Winter: production begins on *A Clockwork Orange*. The film is shot on location in and around London.

1971

Winter: production of *A Clockwork Orange* is completed.

Kubrick edits the film at his home with Bill Butler. Jan Harlan, brother of Kubrick's wife Christiane, works on the film as assistant to the producer.

A Clockwork Orange receives an X rating from the MPAA. In England, the film is restricted to audiences over eighteen.

December 19: *A Clockwork Orange* premieres in New York and San Francisco.

1972

A Clockwork Orange nominated for best picture, Kubrick for best director and adapted screenplay, and Bill Butler for editing.

October: Kubrick withdraws the film and replaces 30 seconds of sexually explicit footage. The film is re-released with an R rating.

1973

Kubrick signs with Warner Bros. to make *Barry Lyndon*, starring Ryan O'Neal and Marisa Berenson, with Jan Harlan as executive producer.

1974

Paths of Glory is finally released in France.

Following violent copycat crimes linked to *A Clockwork Orange*, Kubrick pulls the film from distribution in England.

After six months of shooting in Ireland, filming on *Barry Lyndon* is suspended and the company returns to England, possibly due to bomb threats from the IRA.

1975

Kubrick completes production of *Barry Lyndon* in England.

December 18: *Barry Lyndon* premieres in New York City.

1976

Barry Lyndon is nominated for a best-picture

Oscar as well as Kubrick for best director. The film wins four Oscars: for adapted score, costumes, production design, and cinematography.

February 10: Jan Harlan informs Kubrick of a new hand-held camera stabilizing device, the Steadicam, invented by Garrett Brown.

1977

Kubrick hires novelist Diane Johnson to work with him in adapting Stephen King's *The Shining* as his next film project.

During pre-production for *The Shining*, the Overlook Hotel set is entirely built on a soundstage at EMI-Elstree Studios.

Garrett Brown visits Kubrick to show him the latest model of the Steadicam.

1978

May: shooting begins on *The Shining* with Jan Harlan as executive producer.

Vivian Kubrick films the documentary *Making "The Shining"*.

1979

April: production of *The Shining* at EMI-Elstree is completed.

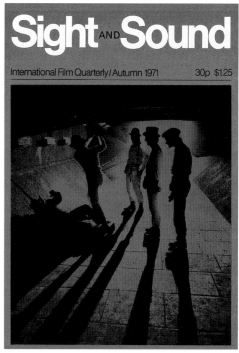

"I have a wife, three children, three dogs, seven cats. I'm not Franz Kafka, sitting alone and suffering."

—SK/1972 (to Craig McGregor)

91 **On the set of** Full Metal Jacket, *which was filmed entirely in England.*
92 **On the set of** A Clockwork Orange.
93 **Pants-on rehearsal for the body cavity search.**

1980
The Kubrick family moves to an estate near St Albans, Herts, where Christiane still lives today.
May 23: *The Shining* opens in New York.

1982
Kubrick options the rights to Brian Aldiss's short story "Super-Toys Last All Summer Long" and hires the writer to work on a screen adaptation.

1985
Kubrick hires Michael Herr to collaborate on the adaptation of Gustav Hasford's Vietnam War novel, *The Short-Timers*.
Locations are selected in surrounding areas of London.
April 23: Kubrick's mother, Gertrude, dies in Los Angeles at age eighty-two.
Summer: Shooting on *Full Metal Jacket* during extremely hot season in England. The actors perform under difficult conditions in full army gear and are surrounded by dirt, rubble, gunfire, and explosions.
October 19: Kubrick's father, Jacques, dies in Los Angeles at age eighty-three.
Fall: post-production on *Full Metal Jacket*.

Vivian Kubrick composes the film's musical score under the name Abigail Mead.

1987
June 26: *Full Metal Jacket* opens in the U.S.. *Full Metal Jacket* receives one Oscar nomination, for best adapted screenplay.

1988
June: Kubrick receives two David di Donatello awards for *Full Metal Jacket*.

1989
Kubrick develops the "Super-Toys" project, briefly working with writer Bob Shaw.

1990
Science-fiction writer Ian Watson is hired to collaborate on the script with Kubrick.

1991
Now known as "A.I.," the project is put on hold.

1993
May: Kubrick in pre-production on "Aryan Papers," a screen adaptation of Louis Begley's Holocaust novel *Wartime Lies*.
Location scouts are sent to Poland, Hungary, and Slovakia.
Warner Bros. puts the project on their release schedule for Christmas 1994.
October: the *Hollywood Reporter* writes that the project was to be shot on location in and around Aarhus, Denmark.
Start date moved to February 1994.
November: Warner Bros. announces Kubrick's next film will be "A.I." and that "Aryan Papers" is postponed.
Artist Chris Baker, known as "Fangorn," is hired to make illustrations of what the futuristic society of "A.I." might look like.

1994
Kubrick brings in writer Sara Maitland to work on "A.I."
December: Frederic Raphael delivers the first draft of an adaptation of Arthur Schnitzler's novel *Traumnovelle*, which would become *Eyes Wide Shut*.

1995
Steven Spielberg visits Kubrick to discuss "A.I."
March: Raphael delivers another draft.
Summer: Kubrick talks with special-effects masters at George Lucas's Industrial Light

and Magic and to effects experts at Quantel concerning "A.I."
December: Warner Bros. press release announces that *Eyes Wide Shut* will start filming in summer 1996. Production of "A.I." is scheduled to follow.
Raphael called to Childwickbury to work on Kubrick's rewrite of the project.

1996
November 7: principal photography begins on *Eyes Wide Shut*.
New York City streets are recreated on the lot at Pinewood Studios in England.

1997
Kubrick receives the Director's Guild of America D. W. Griffith Award for Lifetime Achievement in film directing.
Kubrick receives a Special Golden Lion Award at the Venice Film Festival for his contribution to the art of cinema.

1998
May: Harvey Keitel, cast as Victor Ziegler, leaves the production and is replaced by Sydney Pollack, causing extensive re-shooting. Jennifer Jason Leigh, playing Marion Nathanson, is unavailable for reshooting due to a prior commitment. She is replaced by Marie Richardson.
The original 18-week shooting schedule of *Eyes Wide Shut* stretches to 52 weeks over a period of 15 months.
Eyes Wide Shut announced to open in the autumn, later pushed back.

1999
March 7: Stanley Kubrick dies of a sudden massive heart attack six days after screening the final work print of *Eyes Wide Shut* for Warner Bros.
After the MPAA gives the film an NC-17 rating, Warner Bros. digitally alters the orgy sequences to obtain an R rating for U.S. distribution. The unaltered version of the film is released throughout Europe.
July 16: *Eyes Wide Shut* opens.
The theatrical re-release of *A Clockwork Orange* in Britain marks the first time the film is officially shown there since being withdrawn by Kubrick in 1974.

2001
Jan Harlan's documentary *Stanley Kubrick: A Life in Pictures* premieres at the Berlin Film Festival.
Summer: *Artificial Intelligence: A.I.*, directed by Steven Spielberg, opens. Jan Harlan is the executive producer.
2001: A Space Odyssey re-released.

2002
Stanley Kubrick: A Life in Pictures by Christiane Kubrick is published.

2004
April 18: a traveling exhibition covering Kubrick's life and work first opens, at the Deutsches Filmmuseum in Frankfurt, Germany.

2018
It is reported in the news that Cary Joji Fukunaga will direct Kubrick's "Napoleon" as a six-part series for HBO.